D·E·V·E·L·O·P·I·N·G
ENGLISH
BOOK TWO

GUY DUNBAR · MIKE ROYSTON

Hutchinson

London   Sydney   Auckland   Johannesburg

Hutchinson Education
An imprint of Century Hutchinson Ltd
62–65 Chandos Place, London WC2N 4NW

Century Hutchinson Australia Pty Ltd
89–91 Albion Street, Surry Hills
New South Wales 2010, Australia

Century Hutchinson New Zealand Ltd
32–34 View Road, PO Box 40–086, Glenfield,
Auckland 10, New Zealand

Century Hutchinson South Africa (Pty) Ltd
PO Box 337, Bergvlei 2012, South Africa

First published 1989

Set in Helvetica Light and Plantin
by DP Press Limited, Sevenoaks, Kent
Printed and bound in Great Britain by Scotprint Ltd, Musselburgh

British Library Cataloguing in Publication Data

Dunbar, Guy
 Developing English: a resource book of
 practical activities.
 1. English language — For schools
 I. Title   II. Royston, Mike
 428   PE0000

ISBN 0–09–173191–7

The Publishers' thanks are due to the following
for permission to use photographs: Weston
Mercury/Peter Taylor *page 19;* by kind
permission of Ipswich Town F.C. *pages 21
and 23;* Photo Co-Op *page 29;* Mary Evans
Picture Library *page 95;* Barry Page *pages 76
and 77;* British Museum *page 112;* Photo Co-
Op *page 127.*

Artwork by Juliet Breese, Rob Chapman and
Roy Marchant. Cartoons by Gillies
MacKinnon.

Cover illustration is based on *The Carcase* by Cyril Edward Power, reproduced by
courtesy of Garton and Cooke.

Contents

Acknowledgements

The Publishers' thanks are due to the following for permission to reproduce copyright material:

Unit 1: Murray Pollinger for 'Lucky Break' by Roald Dahl from *The Wonderful World of Henry Sugar*, published by Jonathan Cape and Penguin Books Ltd, copyright © Roald Dahl, 1977; David Higham Associates Ltd for the extract from *Wrong as Usual* by Dorothy Whipple; Andre Deutsch Ltd for the extract from *Albeson and the Germans* by Jan Needle, copyright © Jan Needle, 1977; *Unit 2:* Thompson & Co for the index from *The Topical Times Football Book 1986*; Tim Wood of Oyster Books for the idea for the board game 'Christmas dinner'; *Unit 3:* Thomas Nelson and Sons Ltd for the extracts from 'The Short History of Brian Beck' from *Down Your Way* by Rony Robinson; *Unit 4:* Murray Pollinger for 'The Chant of the Grand Witch' from *The Witches* by Roald Dahl; Collins Publishers for 'Crossing Over' from *Elidor* by Alan Gardner and 'Mixed Brews' by Clive Sampson from *Witches and Charms and Things*; Ian Serraillier for 'The Witch's Cat' from *Happily Ever After*, published by Oxford University Press, copyright © Ian Serraillier, 1963; *Unit 5:* the following for extracts from their newspapers – *The Intelligencer Journal, Aberdeen Press and Journal, The Glasgow Herald, The Times, The Daily Telegraph* and *The Dallas Morning News*; the following for extracts from cover blurbs – Grafton Books, a division of the Collins Publishing Group for *Foiled Again* by W V Butler, Penguin Books Ltd for *Break in the Sun* by Bernard Ashley and *Collision Course* by Nigel Hinton, Hodder and Stoughton for *The Incredible Adventure* by Sheila Burnford, BBC Enterprises Ltd for *Jossy's Giants* by Sid Waddell, Collins Publishers for *The Secret's in the old Attic* by Keene; Jonathan Cape Ltd for the extract from *Run for Your Life* by David Line; *Unit 6:* George Wiedenfeld and Nicolson Ltd for the extract from 'The Snow' from *Poems 1935–1948* by Clifford Dyment; Martin Secker & Warburg Limited for the extract from *For Want of a Nail* by Melvyn Bragg; *Unit 7:* Philip Payne for the extract from *Legend and Drama*; *Unit 8:* Andre Deutsch Ltd for the extract 'George Bunnage' from *The Shirt off a Hanged Man's Back* by Dennis Hamley and 'Nightmare' from *Don't Put Mustard in the Custard* by Michael Rosen; 'Posting Letters' by permission of the author, published by Oxford University Press, copyright © Gregory Harrison; *Unit 10:* Methuen & Co Ltd for lines from 'Winter' by L A G Strong taken from *The Body's Imperfections*; A D Peters for lines from 'Snowscene' by Roger McGough from *Strictly Private*, published by Kestrel Books; Harcourt Brace Jovanovich Ltd for lines from 'Fog' by Carl Sandburg from *Chicago Poems*, copyright © Carl Sandburg, 1944; Angus and Robertson (UK) for 'The Beach' from *The Unceasing Ground* by William Hart Smith; Mrs Lawbury for 'Eagle' from *The Collected Poems* by Andrew Young; Pamela Gillilan for the shape poem 'Invasion'; 'Sky Day Dream' from *Seeing Things*, copyright 1974 by Robert Froman; A D Peters & Co Ltd for 'Cup Final' from *Sky is the Pie* by Roger McGough; 'Townsfolk it is plain' by Meisetu and other Haiku from *An Introduction to Haiku* by Harold G Henderson, copyright © 1958 by Harold G Henderson, reprinted by permission of Doubleday, a division of the Bantam, Doubleday Dell Publishing Group Inc; *Unit 11:* Wes Magee for 'Big Aunt Flo' from *A Fourth Poetry Book* compiled by John Foster and published by Oxford University Press, copyright © Wes Magee, 1981; Penguin Books Ltd for 'Hugger Mugger' from *Hot Dog and Other Poems* by Kit Wright, (Kestrel Books, 1981), copyright © Kit Wright, 1981; Oxford University Press for the extract from *Terry on the Fence* by Bernard Ashley (1975).

The Publishers have made every effort to clear copyrights and trust that their apologies will be accepted for any errors or omissions. They will be pleased to hear from any copyright holder who has not received due acknowledgement, though where no reply was received to their letters requesting permission, the Publishers have assumed that there was no objection to their using the material.

UNIT 1

In trouble

ACTIVITY 1

It does not pay...

What you do Read 'It does not pay . . .' on the opposite page and answer the questions which follow it.

Why? To look carefully at the way someone describes an incident from their own life.

　　　　To 'read between the lines' — to look for the things that are suggested but not said.

　　　　To try out your ideas with someone else and see if you can agree about an answer.

How?　　　**With a partner**

Read the passage carefully. Look at the questions. Talk about them together and go back through the passage to work out your answers.

　　The questions are about things the writer does not tell directly — but he tells enough for you to be able to work out answers.

　　If you and your partner have different ideas, look carefully at the passage and see if you can agree. You may have good reasons for seeing things differently.

IT DOES NOT PAY . . .

At the age of eight, in 1924, I was sent away to boarding-school in a town called Weston-super-Mare, on the south-west coast of England. Those were days of horror, of fierce discipline, of no talking in the dormitories, no running in the corridors, no untidiness of any sort, no this or that or the other, just rules and still more rules that had to be obeyed. And the fear of the dreaded cane hung over us like the fear of death all the time.

'The headmaster wants to see you in his study.' Words of doom. They sent shivers over the skin of your stomach. But off you went, aged perhaps nine years old, down the long bleak corridors and through an archway that took you into the headmaster's private area where only horrible things happened and the smell of pipe tobacco hung in the air like incense. You stood outside the awful black door . . . You took deep breaths . . . You lifted a hand and knocked softly, once.

'Come in! Ah yes, it's Dahl. Well, Dahl, it's been reported to me that you were talking during prep last night.'

'Please sir, I broke my nib and I was only asking Jenkins if he had another one to lend me.'

'I will not tolerate talking in prep. You know that very well . . . Boys who break rules have to be punished.'

'Sir . . . I . . . I had a bust nib . . . I . . .'

'That is no excuse. I am going to teach you that it does not pay to talk during prep.'

He took a cane . . . that was about three feet long with a little curved handle at one end. It was thin and white and very whippy. 'Bend over and touch your toes. Over there by the window.'

'But sir . . .'

'Don't argue with me, boy. Do as you're told.'

I bent over. Then I waited. He always kept you waiting for about ten seconds, and that was when your knees began to shake.

'Bend lower, boy! Touch your toes!'

I stared at the toecaps of my black shoes and I told myself that any moment now this man was going to bash the cane into me so hard that the whole of my bottom would change colour . . .

Swish! . . . Crack!

Then came the pain. It was unbelievable, unbearable, excruciating. It was as though someone had laid a white hot poker across your backside and pressed hard.

The second stroke would be coming soon and it was as much as you could do to stop putting your hands in the way to ward it off. It was the instinctive reaction. But if you did that, it would break your fingers.

Swish! . . . Crack!

The second one landed right alongside the first and the white-hot poker was pressing deeper and deeper into the skin.

Swish! . . . Crack!

The third stroke was where the pain always reached its peak. It could go no further. There was no way it could get any worse. Any more strokes after that simply *prolonged* the agony. You tried not to cry out. Sometimes you couldn't help it. But whether you were able to remain silent or not, it was impossible to stop the tears. They poured down your cheeks in streams and dripped on to the carpet.

The important thing was never to flinch upwards or straighten up when you were hit. If you did that, you got an extra one.

Slowly, deliberately, taking plenty of time, the headmaster delivered three more strokes, making six in all.

'You may go.' The voice came from a cavern miles away, and you straightened up slowly, agonizingly, and grabbed hold of your burning buttocks with both hands and held them as tight as you could and hopped out of the room on the very tips of your toes.

That cruel cane ruled our lives . . . We were caned for talking in the dormitory after lights out, for talking in class, for bad work, for carving our initials on the desk, for climbing over walls, for slovenly appearance, for flicking paper-clips, for forgetting to change into house-shoes in the evenings, for not hanging up our games clothes, and above all for giving the slightest offence to any master. (They weren't called teachers in those days.) In other other words we were caned for doing everything that it was normal for small boys to do.

Roald Dahl

QUESTIONS

1 What idea of the school do you get from the first paragraph?

2 (a) Why is it so frightening to be told 'The headmaster wants to see you in his study'?
   (b) What idea of the headmaster do you get before actually meeting him in the passage?

3 (a) What 'crime' is Roald supposed to have committed?
   (b) What is his explanation?
   (c) How does the headmaster react to this?

4 Why does the headmaster keep Roald waiting before starting to cane him?

5 Which do you think is the worst time: waiting for the cane, getting it, or afterwards?

6 What does the last paragraph add to the idea of the school that you got in the first paragraph?

Wrong as usual

What you do   Read 'Wrong as Usual', a story about a girl who becomes very frightened during a day in school. Then work out the different reasons the girl has for her feelings.

Why?   To think for yourself about what you read.
   To show your understanding by the questions you *ask* (not answer) about the story.

How?   **On your own**

Read the story carefully. Imagine you are introducing this story to a group of people of your own age. Write down a set of questions to help them understand what the girl is feeling at different points in the story.
   It might be useful to read the story twice: the first time to get a general idea of what is going on, the second time looking particularly at those parts about which you need to ask questions.

WRONG AS USUAL

'Now listen to the answers' said Miss Paton. 'Number one: thirty-five minutes. Number two: forty-seven thousand and eighty-one. Number three . . .'
   My eyes followed my figures in anguish. They were wrong as usual!
   'Hands up those who have eight sums right.'
   A hand went up here and there.
   'Hands up those who have seven right.'
   More hands up.
   'Six right. Five right. Four right . . .'
   It was narrowing down, narrowing down. She would soon come to me. My heart thumped against the edge of the desk.
   'Three sums.'
   I looked at her. Her pinched smile was beginning, the smile that she smiled when she was going to say something clever. Fury seized me. She shouldn't say it.
   'Two sums.'
   I took the plunge. I put my hand up.
   There was a silence.

10

'I said two sums right,' said Miss Paton, clearly and coldly.

My hand remained in the air.

'Have *you* two sums right?'

'Yes,' I said, blushing violently.

Miss Paton leaned forward on her desk and looked piercingly at me.

'But this is a world-shaking event,' she said.

My eyes fell from hers.

'Which are they?'

I bent over my book. This was worse, far worse than admitting to none.

'One and two,' I said at random.

'Ah – one and two,' said Miss Paton. 'More extraordinary than ever. Girls, I beg you to notice that on the sixth of June our genius staggered us by the announcement that she had two sums right.'

I was conscious that they all turned to look at me and that Miss Paton went on talking. But I didn't know what she said. 'So I am to enter two marks for you this morning, am I?' I found her saying later, her pen poised over the register like that of a recording angel.

I nodded.

The bell rang. She gathered up her books and left the room. But her going brought me no relief. I knew I should be found out . . .

Lesson succeeded lesson. The morning dragged on.

The last bell rang . . . Perhaps I was going to escape after all . . .

Outside the classroom stretched the shining floor of the great hall. Once let me get across that . . . I saw, with a leap of the heart, that the headmistress was standing at the door of her room, with dignity and folded hands. I hurried in the file, jostling the girl in front of me. Let me get past . . . only let me get past and I would run all the way home and never come back.

But my name was called out. I left the file and walked across to her room.

'Close the door,' she said.

I closed myself in with her. On her desk my exercise book lay open with the sums exposed. Somebody must have taken it from my desk during break.

'This is your exercise book, is it not?'

I nodded . . .

'This morning, in the arithmetic lesson, you said you had two sums right, but you had no sums right and you knew it, didn't you?'

I nodded.

'So you are a cheat?' said the headmistress.

I nodded again. I was a cheat. I submitted to the shame as a dog submits to the tying of a dead hen round his neck.

'You will have to be watched,' said the headmistress, who was no doubt annoyed by my silence. 'And if I have any further complaint, it will be serious. You have been warned.'

I nodded in acceptance.

'You may go,' she said.   *Dorothy Whipple*

I went.

It is DISGUSTING

What you do Read 'It is disgusting' on pages 13–16. The passage is taken from a novel. Stop from time to time to think about it and jot down your thoughts, feelings and ideas about what you are reading.

Why? To think carefully about the ways you react to a story.
To compare your reactions with those of someone else.
To become better at asking questions about stories.
To find out which are the most useful questions to ask.

How? **On your own**

Read the passage. As you read, stop from time to time and think:

- What is going on?
- What has happened?
- What is going to happen next?
- What picture of this scene or character have I got?
- How do I feel about this character?
- How would *I* feel if I were in this situation?

Jot down whatever thoughts, ideas or feelings come into your mind. You need not write much – but make sure you write enough for you to be able to recall your thoughts clearly later.

At the end of the passage, there are instructions for how you can talk about your ideas with a partner.

IT IS DISGUSTING

When Mr Johnson walked onto the platform the spell of silence wavered. There was a low sigh, a gasp of fearful wonder from the body of the hall. Mr Johnson was carrying a long, thin cane with a bent handle. A real cane, not the bamboo stick he kept on his wall. His face looked like stone. As he stared bleakly out at the sea of faces the sigh faded away. He stared and stared, the only movement in the hall his big bony hands flexing themselves round the prayer desk. The cane stuck out from one hand, pointing to the roof, quivering. The silence crept back.

'In this hall,' said Mr Johnson, 'there sits a boy or boys who will shortly be getting a taste of this.'

With a shockingly sudden movement he threw his right hand towards the back wall with enormous force. There was a whistle, a definite, high-pitched whistle, as the cane whipped through the air. From the hall there came another sigh, deeper and more hopeless than the first. It was like a groan. Albeson couldn't take his eyes off the cane, hanging now beside the headmaster's leg. It was so thin, so wickedly thin.

'And that, my fine young friends, is without doubt far and away the pleasantest thing that will happen to them.'

Mr Johnson bared his teeth in a sort of smile that made Albeson lick his lips. 'For when I have finished with that boy, or those boys,' he went on, in a slow, deep voice, 'he or they will be handed over to Her Majesty's police. In my long experience of such matters, I feel quite confident that those gentlemen will know what to do next. And after *that* there will be courts, magistrates, judges and juries – and the final awful clang as the prison gates close.'

He paused and leaned forward, his eyes boring into the children like hot pokers. He dropped his voice to a terrifying hiss.

'Those gates,' he said slowly, 'will not reopen for a very long time. A very . . . long . . . time . . . indeed.'

The children leaned forward as if they had been hypnotized. They stared into Mr Johnson's face. He stared back for long moments.

'For those of you who are not guilty,' he went on at last, 'I had better explain. Over the weekend this school was entered by a gang – I shall assume there were more than one of them from the amount of mindless destruction wrought – by a gang of half-witted oafs who went on a spree of vandalism. If any boy or girl moves so much as a muscle to look now I will beat them, but you will doubtless have noticed certain evidences of this hooliganism. In the classrooms, some of which will be unusable until extensive – and expensive – repair works have been carried out, the destruction was even more marked. And not only the fabric of our school has been damaged. The very heart of it, the soul of Church Street, has been violated and besmirched.'

Mr Johnson clenched his teeth with a snap and his eyes bulged. Albeson had no idea what the words meant, but he could not tear away his gaze. His mouth hung open. Mr Johnson went slowly red. The colour deepened until he was frighteningly purple. The muscles in his cheeks worked.

He let out his breath in a roar that shook the windows.

'It is DISGUSTING!'

This time there was not even a ripple of sound. A dead pause, silent except for the headmaster's breath, rasping and horrible. After a few seconds a girl in the babies started to whimper. A teacher shushed but it was no good. The whimper became a wail. As the little girl began to cry several others joined in, until there was a little bawling bunch in the middle of the hall. For Albeson and the older children it was terrible. The desire to cry, to join in, was overpowering. Albeson bit his lip and squeezed his eyes shut, fighting the tears with everything he'd got.

By the time the crying babies had been led out, Mr Johnson had gone back to normal. But he had not finished with them by a long chalk.

'As you all know,' he said, 'this is not the first time such goings-on have been recorded. I had cause to lecture you before, and that time I warned of the terrible consequences if it should ever happen again. Well, not only has it happened, but it has been done in such a way that the earlier incidents seem relatively minor. The country-dance room has been wrecked, the hall has been turned into a filthy den, and every classroom has in some way been damaged. Apart from anything else, my friends, the culprits will be faced with a bill running into hundreds, possibly thousands, of pounds.'

Some of the braver boys felt able to make noises of surprise now that the squalling babies had eased the tension. But Mr Johnson slammed the side of the desk with his cane. They shut up.

'There are some things that money cannot buy, however,' Mr Johnson went on. 'You children may have cats and dogs, some of you. Others may have white mice or guinea-pigs. Some of the teachers in this school let you pet, or stroke, or look at animals from time to time. I believe it is a good thing. We should all love living creatures, great or small. It is God's law.'

The strain was back. There was a new feeling of uncomfortableness now that God had been brought into it. Albeson's tongue moved on his lips once more.

'In Mrs Armstrong's class there was a tank of fish. Tropical fish of great worth and great beauty. She tells me that many of you spent many hours watching them. Mrs Armstrong loved her little fish very much.'

The headmaster paused. He seemed about to go red again, to shake with rage. Then he shrugged.

'I say "was" with meaning. For these filthy little oafs smashed that fish tank and killed the little fishes. Yes. Some boys sitting in front of me today left Mrs Armstrong's fish to flap and suffocate on the classroom floor. What do we think of that, eh?'

Whatever anyone else felt, Albeson felt awful. He knew his face was bright red. He wanted to die. But all round him other faces were red, other children

14

shuffled guiltily on their haunches. It seemed that in some strange way everyone felt ashamed, everyone felt it had been them. Albeson had a vision of Smithie's blood-filled shoe leaking slowly into the pool of water. Little oafs, breaking God's law.

'Today, boys and girls,' said Mr Johnson, 'I am going to call in the police. I expect you will all know the term C.I.D. from your television viewing. It is short for Criminal Investigation Department. Today the Criminal Investigation Department of the city police will be sending along some detectives. As you can imagine, the culprits will be found in very short order. Then this disgusting business will be made an end of for good and all.'

He paused for quite a time to let the news sink in. People were beginning to look seriously frightened now. There were whimpers coming from several of the older girls and a lot of white faces among the top boys. Mr Johnson rapped his knuckles on the desk in a brisk, business-like way.

'There is one way we can avoid all this nastiness,' he said. 'The culprits can give themselves up. The results for them will be just the same in the end; they must be punished. But the police, and the magistrates, and the education authorities, are bound to take into account a truthful and courageous act, however late it is in coming. I can say with all truthfulness that it would be better for everybody if the boys concerned will own up.'

There was a general shuffling. Some people looked around them, others stared at the floor. At least half the children looked as though they had done it. Even some of the teachers seemed very ill at ease. After a minute the headmaster spoke again.

'I will make one more plea for honesty,' he said. 'And I will also make an offer. If the culprits will stand up here and now I will not cane them. They must face the consequences of their acts of course. But the first part of their punishment I will drop.' He waved the cane so that it swished gently. 'You have two minutes,' he said.

Jan Needle

With a partner

Go back over the passage and use your notes to talk about how you reacted to the characters and to the situation in the story. Find out if you felt similar or different things. Talk about the things that now seem important to you.

If you get stuck, some of these ideas may help:

Imagine you are sitting in the front row of the assembly.

- What is your first impression of Mr Johnson?

- What are you thinking has happened?

- What ideas go through your mind when the police and prison are threatened?

- What picture do you get in your mind when you first realize what has been done?

- How do you feel at the end?

- Which part of this passage sticks most in your mind?

- Why does the writer take so long to tell you what has happened?

- What do you make of the Albeson character who is mentioned several times?

16

ACTIVITY 4

Is that for real?

What you do   Talk about the differences and similarities between the three stories you have been working with.

Why?   To bring together and compare your reactions to the three stories.
   To increase your understanding of how the stories work.

How?   **In a group**

Talk about and try to agree answers to the following questions.
   Someone will need to take notes so that the agreements – or disagreements – can be reported back to the rest of the class.

1   Do you think these stories are real or made up? Give reasons for your answer.

2   Do you think it matters whether the stories are real or made up?

3   Which of the three stories do you like most? Which do you like least?

4   What different reasons do the members of your group have for their likes and dislikes?

5   You worked with each of these stories in different ways. Which of these ways did you enjoy most and find most helpful to you?

Your own writing

What you do Talk about some of the frightening and nasty things that have happened to you. Then write a story about them.

Why? To think and talk about events before you use them in a story.

To help you remember — or make up — the details of events.

To practise storytelling before you start writing.

How? **In a group**

Choose one of the following topics. Jot down a few notes to help you sort out your memories — names, places etc. — and put them in order. Make up what you cannot remember. Then tell your story to your group.

- A time when you were punished for something you did not do.

- A time when you deserved punishing but not as much as you were.

- A time when you were bullied by an adult — someone who thought they had the right to do so.

- A time when you were hurt — either deliberately or accidentally.

- A time when you felt really scared of what was going to happen to you.

When each member of the group has told their story, the others should ask questions to help the storyteller get things clearer.

On your own

When everyone has told their story, add anything helpful to your own story notes and write up a version of the story you have just told.

Games and play

Read with speed:
using an index

What you do   Read the Index from a 1986 Football Annual which begins on the opposite page and use it to answer the ten questions below. Then work out five questions of your own for your partner to answer.

Why?   To practise using the Index of a book quickly and correctly.

How?   **On your own**

Look briefly at the Index to see how it is organized. See if you can write down the answers to these ten questions in less than ten minutes.

1   On which page will you find a picture of Joe Jordan?

2   In this book, how many pages contain pictures of Bruce Grobbelaar?

3   For which club does Glenn Roeder play?

4   On which page can you find a picture of a player whose first name is Adrian?

5   There are two players called Miller in this Index. For which teams do they play?

6   In this Index, there are two men with the same surname who are *not* players. Who are they?

7   If there were a player named Smith included in this Index, between which two surnames would his name come?

8   Two players whose surnames begin with the same letter play for Oxford United. Who are they?

9   Why does Remi Moses come *before* Derek Mountfield?

10   There are six letters of the alphabet which do not appear in this Index. Which letters are they?

With a partner

Compare your answers. If you find any disagreements, explain why you got the answer you did. Work out five questions for your partner to answer then check the results.

YOUR PICTURE INDEX

Invent a board game

What you do With a partner, think up a brand-new board game, complete with its own rules and instructions on how to play. Then, using cardboard, paper, crayons and other simple materials, make the game so that other people in your class can enjoy playing it. (An example of a made-up board game is shown on the opposite page.)

Why? To use your imagination to think up your own original board game.

To write the instructions on how to play clearly enough for others to follow.

To read other people's instructions accurately so that you can understand how to play the games *they* have made.

How? **With a partner**

Bring into class a selection of the board games you already have. If any of them are new to your partner, explain the rules, then demonstrate by playing. Talk about the things which board games, roughly speaking, have in common, for example:

- the object of the game and how you win

- how you move round or across the board and what you use to do so (counters, pegs, small objects of various shapes?)

- the shape and lay-out of the board

- when and how the players take their turn

- the obstacles or penalties, bonuses or rewards, there are in the game

- how much skill and how much luck is involved.

Decide on the basic idea for the game you are going to make. The best way to get started is to do a rough sketch of the board and a draft of the main rules. Make your game as attractive as you can. Write up a careful explanation of 'How to Play', making it clear and easy to follow – remember that no one else knows anything about how your game works.

Play your game. Make a note of any details you need to add to the rules to make them clearer. Write a final set of rules, if necessary.

START
1
2
3
4
5

6 MOVE ON 3
7 THROW AGAIN
8
9 MOVE ON 3
10

20
GO BACK TO THE SQUARE YOU WERE ON
21
22
23 MOVE ON 3
24

19 MOVE ON 3
18
17
16
15

33
34
32
31 GO BACK TO SQUARE 12
30 MOVE ON 3
29

RULES – 2 players. You need one counter for each player and a dice. Start on square 1. Throw the dice in turn, moving round the board according to the number shown. If you land on a hazard or bonus square, follow the instructions. First to reach the Christmas Dinner – WINS!

25 THROW AGAIN
26
27
28

14 MOVE ON 3
13
12 GO BACK TO THE SQUARE YOU WERE ON
11

25

I've grown out of them now...

What you do Read 'I've grown out of them now' on the opposite page. It was written by a pupil of your age. Then write a description of some of the games *you* used to play when you were younger. They might be games you played by yourself, or with friends, or both.

Why? To capture in your writing the feelings that come back to you when you remember childhood games.
To give an idea through your writing of the sort of person you were at a younger age.
To *entertain* whoever reads your descriptions.

How? **In a group**

Tell each other about games you most remember playing.

- Why do you remember these particular games?
- Did people in your group play exactly the same games, or versions of the same games? In other words, did any of your friends follow different rules or chant different words?
- Does the passage on the opposite page make you remember any of your own 'pretend' games?
- Did you play any games which involved chasing, hiding or paying 'forfeits'?
- Did you play any 'dare' games?
- Did you play any games with friends where you used special words or phrases?
- Were there any games which involved tricking or annoying adults?

On your own

Choose two or three of your favourite childhood games to write about. It might be a good idea to choose games that are quite different from each other, for the sake of variety.
If you wish, do some drawings to help the reader catch the 'mood' of the games you describe.

I'VE GROWN OUT OF THEM NOW . . .

Jigsaws really bore me, but what else is there to do on a rainy day? Mum's ideas usually run as far as 'tidy up your room'. How exciting! What a pity I'm too old now to do the things I enjoyed when I was younger . . .

One game I used to love playing was 'Restaurants'. In our garden we have a shed on a square of concrete. The shed was where I cooked the food. I went all the way with this game. I even had my dolls as customers and Ted – named Bonzo – as the big fat rich man who sat in a corner and ordered the best food in the restaurant.

The toys used to sit around the tables, which were made of cardboard boxes. I gave them all some ripped-up pieces of paper to pay for their food. They didn't have a lot of choice on the menu. There was fish and chips, sausage and chips, bacon and chips, or just chips. Luckily, they all loved chips. I would take their orders and rush off to the shed to cook them, muttering to myself about how busy I was – just like my Mum does!

Once inside the shed, the work really began. For instance, the chips had to be cut up out of newspaper. The rich toys, like Bonzo, could afford wine. They even had a choice – red or white. Red was water in a coke bottle with red paint on the outside. I then had to fry the chips, in a real chip-pan which I 'borrowed' from the kitchen when Mum wasn't looking. I had a toy cooker as well.

At that time in my life, my ambition was to be a waitress – until I found another game to play. At the bottom of our garden we have a sunhouse. It's in the corner of the garden with prickly thorn bushes just outside the door and grass underneath it.

I used it as a boat. At the weekends, I would sail on my boat, usually round the world. I had an old steering-wheel on a long wooden handle. The end of the handle was placed in a bottle. The only thing my boat didn't have was a proper sea. This little detail didn't really bother me as the long grass could soon turn into choppy waves, especially when a good breeze was blowing. Mind you, it did get a bit scary when the sea was rough. I enjoyed walking on the tiny ledge outside the sunhouse, about six inches in diameter. I was always careful not to fall into the prickly thorns, since I knew they were really sharks.

After finishing that game, I used to rush inside to Mum and announce that I wanted to be 'a sailor girl'. I'm glad to say, though, that my ambition is now a bit more sensible. I want to become a nursery nurse, which probably goes back to the time I used to play hospitals with two of my friends from junior school . . . but that's another story.

Alison

27

A beginner's guide

What you do Choose a sport which you play and/or know a lot about. Make a booklet for people who are interested in taking up this sport as 'beginners'.

Why? To get across basic facts, information and advice in an easy-to-understand way.

To work out exactly *what* the readers of your booklet need to know and, from this, to find the most helpful ways of telling them.

To design a booklet which is attractively laid out, so that people will enjoy using it as they learn.

How? **On your own**

Think first of the different *sections* your booklet might have, then of the best order to put them in. This will depend on the sport you have chosen, but included in your section headings could be:

- **Rules of the Game** - **Training** - **Tactics** - **Equipment**

- **Improving your skills** - **How to join a club** - **Competitions you can enter**

You can break down these main headings into more detailed parts later on.

Decide on the most helpful and attractive lay-out for your booklet:

- What size and shape do you want it to be?

- How are you going to set out each of the pages?

- What is your front cover going to be like?

It will help if you use diagrams and drawings as much as possible to go along with your writing.

*Note:*There is no reason why you should not choose to write your booklet about a well-known sport. However, if you *do* know about a less common sport it might be that more people will want to read it out of curiosity. (One class produced booklets about: Judo; Modern Rhythmic Gymnastics; American Football; Uni-Hock; Squash; Orienteering; Pool; BMX racing; Archery; Coarse Fishing; Water Polo; Basketball; Badminton; Synchronised Swimming.)

28

Friends

The trouble with friends

What you do Read aloud two passages from the play. 'The Short History of Brian Beck'. They tell about Brian and his friends: the first passage describes a birthday party, the second an incident at junior school.

Choose two occasions in your own life when you have had problems with friends. Write about them in the form of a play like the one you have just read.

Why? To act a character in a play by reading aloud.

To practise writing in a form which may be new (or fairly new) to you.

To bring out people's characters and feelings by what you give them to say.

How? **As a class**

Read the 'Brian Beck' scenes. There are sixteen characters, so it is best to read the scenes as a class.

On your own

For the two scenes of your own play, bring to mind any times in your life, recently or when you were much younger, which show you and your friends falling out, disagreeing or finding it difficult to get on together. The occasions need not be really important ones: the point of this activity is to put down on paper in a *realistic* way the things that people say at such times.

Now make these important decisions:

- Apart from yourself, how many people are you going to have in each scene?
- How are the scenes going to begin and end?
- How are you going to make clear where each scene is taking place?
- Are you going to have a Narrator as in the 'Brian Beck' play?

Draft your two scenes. Then read them aloud, playing all the parts yourself. You will probably need several tries before you get the characters sounding really true-to-life.

Finally, write up your scenes, setting them out as in the play you have read. If you have margins on your paper, it is helpful to use them for the names of the speakers.

THE SHORT HISTORY OF BRIAN BECK:
Extract 1

Narrator: Brian wasn't very good at school. He was more interested in football. And pennies-up-the-wall. And running. And fighting. And girls, of course. He first took an interest in a girl at the age of six and a half. Her name was Marjorie Otter.

(Ball bouncing)

Marjorie: Let's have a kick.

Brian: No. Football's a boy's game. You're not a boy.

Marjorie: I wish I was.

Brian: Well, you're not.

Marjorie: Boys have all the fun.

Brian: They don't.

Marjorie: Yes, they do.

Brian: They don't. I know. I've got three sisters.

Marjorie: You haven't.

Brian: Yes, I have.

Marjorie: Haven't.

Brian: Have.

Marjorie: *(Raising voice)* Haven't!

Brian: *(Slapping her)* Have! Have! Have! Have!

Miss Glatt: Now, what's all this? Brian Beck! We don't have fighting in this school. You'd better come with me. Fighting with girls, too!

Narrator: But when Marjorie had her seventh birthday party she invited 'Master Brian Beck'.

Brian: I've got a letter! I've got a letter! A real one! Come through the door. With a stamp. Dad! Look!

Father: If it's like the letters I get, it will be a bill. Give it back to the postman.

Brian: Who's written a letter to me? Look, it says, here, my name.

Father: Open it and read it, then you will know.

Brian:.   I can't. Look it's a card, not a letter. What's it say?

Mother: 'Marjorie Otter invites Brian Beck to her birthday party on Saturday, June the 11th, at 4 o'clock. RSVP.'

Brian: It's from her. I'm not going to *her* party.

Mother: Yes, you are. This is an invitation. You have to reply. That's what RSVP means.

Brian: I don't like her! I'm not going to her party.

Father: She's got you in her grip, son. It's no use fighting women. She's caught you, I'm afraid.

Brian: I'm not going to her party.

Narrator: And so Brian dressed in his best red trousers and went to the party.

(Knock at the door)

Mother: Hello, Mrs Otter. I've brought Brian.

Brian: I'm not going in there! I want to go home!

Mrs Otter: Hello, Brian. Come in. The party's just started.

Brian: I'm not going in there.

Mrs Otter: Doesn't he look nice, Mrs Beck? He's very smart, isn't he!

Brian: I'm going home.

Narrator: And when he got into the party, he joined all the others who had jammed into the kitchen to eat.

John: Strawberry mousse, with real strawberries on the top.

Graham: Mint ice cream with bits of chocolate in it, and a wafer.

David: Lemon curd sandwiches.

Jennifer: Sausages on sticks.

Marjorie: My birthday cake with candle wax all over the icing.

John: And sausage rolls.

Jennifer: And fish paste sandwiches, that nobody likes.

Angela: And mud pie! And cowpat roll! And frogspawn jelly!

Marjorie: Mum, stop her. Listen to what Angela's saying. Stop her, mum!

Narrator: And after the food everyone played games. Angela kissed Brian in *Postman's Knock* and Marjorie hit her. Angela kissed Brian when there wasn't *Postman's Knock*. Angela told her friends that she loved Brian.

Angela: I love Brian.

Narrator: And Marjorie cried, and everyone else laughed or shouted. The boys began to fight, the girls squealed and someone was sick. Mrs Otter stopped the party and everyone went home.

(A girl crying)

Extract 2
(Brian is now ten)

Narrator: He got tonsilitis. And appendicitis. And toothache. And earache. And trouble at school. Trouble at school was the worst of everything he ever got. There was a new teacher called Mr Barrett. Mr Barrett hated litter, and all forms of untidiness.

Mr Barrett: You're ten years old, Brian Beck, and you sit there dropping paper on the floor. Look at the mess!

Brian: It isn't all mine, sir.

Mr Barrett: Isn't it, lad? It's all round your desk. Did anyone else put this litter under this lad's desk?

Boys and girls: No, sir.

Mr Barrett: Then it must be yours, boy.

Brian: It's not, sir. Not all of it.

Mr Barrett: Then all these other boys and girls are liars? Is that what you're trying to tell me? Well, I can see I shall have to watch you, calling people liars and dropping litter! Go and sit by my desk!

Narrator: And after that first fight about litter, everything slowly got worse.

Mr Barrett: Just look at your hair, boy. What a state to come to school in!

Narrator: Brian found it hard to get anything right. His sums went wrong. And his spellings. And his writing. And even his pictures.

Mr Barrett: Just look at this disgraceful mess. All this paint and water. What a disgusting mess, lad!

Brian: Sorry, sir.

Mr Barrett: Being sorry's no good, lad, if you don't try to make things better.

Brian: No, sir. Sorry, sir.

Narrator: And Brian even came to hate Mr Barrett. He had never hated anyone in all his life before. But Mr Barrett was making school terrible for him. Brian lay in bed at nights wondering how he could possibly get free from Mr Barrett.

Brian: Wood shavings in his playtime tea? Polish on the soles of his shoes, so he slips? A sharpened ruler to stick in his ear?

Narrator: The other children took the hint from Mr Barrett. Brian Beck was not a nice boy to play with any more.

Graham: You're silly, Brian Beck. Not playing with you!

Jennifer: Ooooh. We don't want to play with a boy who's scruffy like you.

Angela: You smell, Brian Beck. We're not sitting next to you.

David: Thick as a plank of wood you are. Mr Barrett says so!

Marjorie: You can't do anything right, Brian Beck!

Narrator: When even Marjorie turned against him, Brian gave up. He decided to leave home. He packed a handkerchief and stuck it on a stick and set off for Scotland.

Policeman: We found your boy walking about near the station, Mrs Beck. He says he's seventeen years old and has left home.

Mother: He's ten. Look at him, officer, and you can see that. Now stop crying, Brian. That's not going to help.

Policeman: I gave him a cup of tea at the station, Mrs Beck. And a chocolate biscuit. But he kept trying to say something about a Mr Barrett. Does it make any sense to you?

Rony Robinson

Penfriend

What you do Imagine that one of your best friends moved away from your district to another part of the country a few months ago. He/she has sent you a letter and has asked you to write back, giving all the news about what has been happening to you, other friends, school, etc.

Write your letter in reply.

Why? To practise planning, setting out and writing a 'friendly' letter.

To bring out the character of both yourself and your friend by the way you write.

How? **On your own**

Imagine your 'penfriend' to be one of your *real* friends and make the news you send true.

Read the letter on the opposite page. It will show you how to set out a letter and may give you some ideas for what to write about.

Plan your letter carefully so that it has clear paragraphs – although it is a 'friendly' rather than a 'formal' letter, it should not ramble on and on!

Finally, show your letter to the friend you have imagined writing to. Is it the kind of letter they would enjoy reading if they really had moved away?

16 Daleway Road
Exton
July 5th 1988.

Dear Tony,
    Don't die of shock! I've been meaning to reply to your letter every day, but have kept finding more interesting things to do instead (joke). Your new house sounds great - I envy you being near the sea, and especially having your own bedroom. Your new school sounds OK as well, in spite of all the tests and exams you've been having. So have we! I'm not going to tell you how brilliantly I did in case I depress you. At least you've got a decent soccer team, unlike our useless lot which ended the season still losing (surprise, surprise!).

    I'd better tell you the most important news first. Our house got burgled last Tuesday night! It must have happened when we were all asleep. When dad went down to get in the milk he found most of the drawers in the lounge tipped out. Things were scattered all over the floor. It didn't half look a mess. We phoned for the police, and a couple of Panda-cars came round. Then some bloke from the CID arrived, taking statements and looking for finger prints. Nobody's been caught yet.

    Everybody at school says hello. Karen is still pining away with love for you. She told me to send five hundred of her best kisses. (She didn't really, but I thought it would make you blush!) Andy said I have to remind you that you still owe him 67p from the time we went to Alton Towers and you lost your money.

    I'd better stop now. I've still got some homework to do (groan-History) Thanks for the invitation to come and see you in the holidays. Mum says I can. Can we fix up the details next time I write? The middle of August sounds a pretty good time, if it's OK with you.
I still miss having you around (honest!) Bri

The best of friends?

What you do Use copies of the 'score-sheet' on the opposite page to help you discuss in a group 'What Makes a Good Friend'.

Why? To talk about how and why you get on with people of your own age.
   To share your ideas with the group so that you have to think about opinions other than your own.

How? **On your own**

Work your way through the ten items in the list on the opposite page. Take them in a different order from that printed if you wish.
   Although you are part of a group, the 'scores' you give will be your own: they show what *you* think are the qualities that make a good friend.

In a group

As you put forward your opinions about the things on the list, give *reasons* for what you think. Often, the best reasons will stem from things that have actually happened between you and your friends, so tell the other members of the group as much about these as possible.
   When you have talked your way through the list, think of any qualities you look for in a friend which are not mentioned. Add these to the list and show how important you think they are by the scores you give them.

WHAT MAKES A GOOD FRIEND?

Below is a list of ten different ideas about what makes a good friend.

Consider each one, and then use the space on the right-hand side to give it a personal 'score' out of ten, using the following system:

10 means 'an excellent quality in a friend'

8 or 9 means 'a very good quality'

6 or 7 means 'average'

4 or 5 means 'poor'

2 or 3 means 'a bad quality in a friend'

Below 2 means 'a quality I would never want in a friend'

1   A friend is someone who shares your tastes in things and has the same interests – for example, in music, clothes, sport, etc. ☐

2   A friend is someone who will back you up in an argument or fight, whatever the 'rights' and 'wrongs' of the situation. ☐

3   A friend is someone who shares your sense of humour. ☐

4   A friend is someone you can confide in, knowing that they will not 'tell tales' to others afterwards. ☐

5   A friend is someone who is approved of by your family. ☐

6   A friend is someone who would lie for you to get you out of trouble at school or at home. ☐

7   A friend is someone who has a high opinion of you. ☐

8   A friend is someone you can rely on to help you out when you are in difficulties – say, when you need help with homework or when you need to borrow money. ☐

9   A friend is someone who will always cheer you up when you are feeling 'down' or depressed. ☐

10   A friend is someone whom you look up to or admire for certain qualities they have. ☐

UNIT 4

Witchcraft

Performing a witches' chant

What you do   In a group, perform Roald Dahl's 'The Chant of the Grand High Witch' on pages 42 and 43.

Rehearse your performance carefully, then put it on tape.

Why?   To get across the feeling of the chant by using various combinations of voices, giving special attention to sound and rhythm.

To experiment with the possibilities of tape-recording in order to add variety to your performance.

How?   **In a group**

The best group size for this Activity is ten to twelve.

Read through 'The Chant of the Grand High Witch' to yourself. Notice that, as well as the witches, there are the voices of a number of children and teachers. Sometimes single voices are heard, sometimes voices speaking together.

Decide between you on the following things:

● how many different voices you will have and who will do them

● what *accents* you are going to use

● which words you want to emphasize and how they should sound

● where to be loud and where to be quieter

● where to pause and for how long

● where to go fast and where to go more slowly.

Try out your performance on tape. Listen carefully to the result. Agree on what needs to be changed, taken out, put in or improved.

Finally, do a taped performance which has as much expression as you can put into it. Don't be satisfied until it sounds *exactly* right.

THE CHANT OF THE GRAND HIGH WITCH

'Down with children! Do them in!
Boil their bones and fry their skin!
Bish them, sqvish them, bash them, mash them!
Brrreak them, shake them, slash them, smash
them!
Offer chocs vith magic powder!
Say 'Eat up!' then say it louder.
Crrram them full of sticky eats,
Send them home still guzzling sveets.
And in the morning little fools
Go marching off to separate schools.
A girl feels sick and goes all pale.
She yells, 'Hey, look! I've grrrown a tail!'
A boy who's standing next to her
Screams, 'Help, I think I'm growing fur!'
Another shouts, 'Ve look like frrreaks!'
There's viskers growing on our cheeks!'
A boy who vos extremely tall
Cries out, 'Vot's wrong? I'm grrrowing small!'
Four tiny legs begin to sprrrout
From everybody rrround about.
There are no children! only MICE!
In every school is mice galore
All rrrunning rrround the school-rrroom floor!
And all the poor demented teachers
Is yelling, 'Hey, who are these crrreatures?'
They stand upon the desks and shout,
'Get out, you filthy mice! Get out!
Vill someone fetch some mouse-trrraps please!
And don't forget to bring the cheese!'
Now mouse-trrraps come and every trrrap
Goes snippy-snip and snappy-snap.
The mouse-trrraps have a powerful spring,
The springs go crack and snap and ping!
Is lovely noise for us to hear!
Is music to a vitch's ear!

Dead mice is every place arrround
Piled two feet deep upon the grrround,
Vith teachers searching left and right,
But not a single child in sight!
The teachers cry, 'Vot's going on?
Oh vhere have all the children gone?
Is half-past nine and as a rrrule
They're never late as this for school!'
Poor teachers don't know vot to do
Some sit and rrread, and just a few
Amuse themselves throughout the day
By sweeping all the mice away.
AND ALL US VITCHES SHOUT 'HOORAY'!

Roald Dahl

Reading between the lines

What you do   Read the passage 'Crossing Over' which begins on the opposite page. It comes from Alan Garner's novel *Elidor*.

Answer in writing a number of questions on the passage. Then in a group, talk about what you have written with other people, comparing your ideas and opinions with theirs.

Why?   To see how the writer builds up a strong atmosphere suited to what is being described.

To think about how things are *suggested* but not directly stated by the writer in order to create a feeling of strangeness.

To share your own responses to the passage with other people and explain/defend what you think where there are differences of opinion.

How?   **On your own**

Read the passage carefully, twice. Write your answers to the questions which follow it. These questions are meant to get you thinking about your *own* responses: they do not have 'right' and 'wrong' answers. (How you go on to work in your group is explained at the end of the passage.)

Before starting, you need to know that four children – Roland, Nick, Helen and David – have wandered into an area of the city which is being demolished. Nearby, a blind fiddler has been playing strange music. They have been playing football with a plastic ball, but when Roland kicked it it soared high, as if carried on a note from the violin, and smashed a window high up in a ruined church.

Helen and David have gone in to look for the ball. Nick has followed them. Since none of them has come back, Roland decides to go into the church as well . . .

CROSSING OVER

Roland went through into the body of the church.

The floor boards and joists had been taken away, leaving the bare earth: everything movable had been ripped out down to the brick. The church was a cavern. Above Roland's head the three lancets of the west window glowed like orange candles against the fading light. The middle lancet, the tallest, was shattered, and the glass lay on the earth. But there was no ball.

'Nick! Helen! David! Where are you?'

The dust hung like mist in the church.

Roland went back to the passage. At the end was a staircase. The bannisters had been pulled out, but the steps remained.

'David! Nick! Come down: please don't hide! I don't like it!'

No one answered. Roland's footsteps thumped on the stairs. Two rooms opened off a landing at the top, and both were empty.

'Nick!'

The echo filled the church.

'Nick!'

Round and round, his voice went, and through it came a noise. It was low and vibrant, like wind in a chimney. It grew louder, more taut, and the wall blurred, and the floor shook. The noise was in the fabric of the church: it pulsed with sound. Then he heard a heavy door open, and close; the noise faded away. It was now too still in the church, and footsteps were moving over the rubble in the passage downstairs.

'Who's there?' said Roland.

The footsteps reached the stairs and began to climb.

'Who's there?'

'Do not be afraid,' said a voice.

'Who are you? What do you want?'

The footsteps were at the top of the stairs. A shadow fell across the landing.

'No!' cried Roland. 'Don't come any nearer!'

The fiddler stood in the doorway.

'I shall not harm you. Take the end of my bow, and lead me. The stairs are dangerous.'

He was bent and thin: he limped; his voice was old: there looked to be no strength in him: and he was between Roland and the stairs. He stretched out his fiddle bow.

'Help me.'

'All – all right.'

Roland put his hand forward to take the bow, but as he was about to touch it a shock struck his fingertips, driving light through his forehead between the eyes. It was as though a shutter had been lifted in his mind, and in the moment before it dropped again he saw something; but it went so quickly that all he could hold was the shape of its emptiness.

'What did you see?'

'See? I didn't – see. I – through my fingers – . See? Towers – like flame. – A candle in darkness. – A black wind.'

'Lead me.'

'Yes.'

Roland went down the stairs, a step at a time, dazed but no longer frightened. The church was somehow remote from him now, and flat, like a piece of stage scenery. The only real things were the fiddler and his bow.

'I heard your music,' said Roland. 'Why were you playing so far away from people?'

'I was near you. Are you not people?' They had reached the bottom of the stairs, and were standing on the earth floor of the church. 'Give me my bow.'

'I can't stay,' said Roland. But the old man put the fiddle to his shoulder. 'I am looking for my sister and my two brothers –' The old man began to play. '– and I must find them before dark –' It was the wild dance he had heard before. '– and we've a train to catch. What's that noise? – Stop! – It's hurting! – Please! –'

The air took up the fiddler's note. It was the sound Roland had heard upstairs, but now it was louder, building waves that jarred the church, and went through Roland's body until he felt he was threaded on the sound.

'– Please! –'

'Now! Open the door!'

'I can't! It's locked!'

'Open it! There is little time!'

'But – !'

'Now!'

Roland stumbled to the door, grasped the iron handle, and pulled with all his weight. The door opened, and he ran out on to the cobbles of the street, head down, driven by the noise.

But he never reached the far pavement, for the cobbles were moving under him. He turned. The outline of the church rippled in the air and vanished. He was standing among boulders on a sea-shore, and the music died into the crash of breakers, and the long fall of surf.

Alan Garner

46

QUESTIONS

1 Give your own idea of what the inside of the church is like.

2 Remember that the three children with Roland – they are actually his sister and two brothers – have gone into the building before him. What do you imagine Roland's thoughts and feelings are as he looks around the church?

3 After the noise, there is a silence, then footsteps. What does this lead *you* to expect?

4 What do you suppose Roland is thinking as the footsteps approach him?

5 What happens to Roland, do you think, when he touches the fiddler's bow?

6 (a) What seems to stop Roland from getting away from the fiddler and forces him to do what the fiddler wants him to?
  (b) What do you think is the explanation behind this?

7 (a) What impression of the fiddler do you get?
  (b) Does your impression of him stay the same all through the passage?

8 What do you think is happening at the end?

In a group

Discuss what each of you has written. Listen to one another's ideas and see where you agree and disagree,

If there are different points of view and opinions, go back to the passage to check. Remember that there may well be several ways of seeing the same thing.

Witches' charms

What you do Read the three traditional English charms on the opposite page. Such charms were usually meant to cure something, protect people from something nasty, or get rid of something/someone which/who was causing trouble.

Invent several charms of your own to do similar things. Write them out and illustrate them suitably for a class display.

Why? To amuse yourself and your readers.

To let your imagination run riot producing the nastiest, most horrible ideas you can think of.

How? **On your own**

Decide what you want your charms to do.

You might want to *cure* yourself of such things as: athlete's foot, biting your nails, having to get up on Sunday morning, not being able to do French/Maths/Needlework, etc.

You might want to *protect* yourself from: school dinners, your big brother/sister, your teacher, homework, the record you hate most, etc.

You might want to *get rid of:* school, wax in your ears, your little brother/sister, your next-door neighbour's dog, etc.

Write the charms in whatever style you wish. It sometimes makes them sound more nasty if you use the kind of 'old-fashioned' language in the examples on the opposite page. (Not all the words need make sense: it's mainly their *sounds* that are flesh-creeping.)

A Charm to Extract a Tooth Without Pain.

Take some newts, by some called lizards, and those nasty beetles which are found in ferns in the summer time. Calcine them in an iron pot and make a powder thereof. Wet the forefinger of the right hand and insert it in the powder, then apply it to the tooth frequently, refraining from spitting it off, when the tooth will fall away without pain. It is proven.

Charm To Make a Cordiall Broth.

Take three sheep's hinges with the wool of their heads. Take also three dozen of sheep's trotters; the livers of two bullocks, with half a peck of oatmeal. Boyl these together in a cauldron for two hours, then strain the Broth through a hair sack-cloth and leave to cool. The use of it then is to appease a grumbling in the gut, or wambling stomach, by drinking one Pot at a time and eating the meat after it. This will preserve you from hunger and wind in the stomack, using it but once in two hours.

Charm To Prevent Stiffening of the Bones.

Take thirty snails found in the garden and earthworms of middling size to a similar number. Bruise the snails and wash them and the worms in fair waters. Cut the worms into pieces. Boyl these in a piece of spring water to a pint. Pour it boyling onto two ounces of eringo root candied and sliced thin. When it is cold, strain it through a fine flannel bag. Take a quarter of it, warmed with an equal quantity of Cow's milk till well, at twilight.

Rhythm and rhyme

What you do Read the three poems 'Queen Nefertiti', 'Mixed Brews' and 'The Witch's Cat'.

Parts of each poem have been printed differently from the way the poets wrote them.

Decide what the poets *really* wrote and how they set it out.

Why? To think about the reasons why poets arrange words and lines in particular patterns.

To think about the reasons for preferring one word to another when writing poetry.

To develop your own ideas by discussing them with another person.

How? **With a partner**

There are three stages to this Activity. Work through them in the following order:

1 The first and last verses of the poem below have been printed as the poet wrote them. However, the middle *three* verses have been printed as if they were prose.

Put the lines back as you think the poet meant them to be. Write down what you decide on a sheet of paper. Make use of all the clues you can, especially the rhyme and rhythm.

QUEEN NEFERTITI

Spin a coin, spin a coin,
All fall down;
Queen Nefertiti
Stalks through the town.

Over the pavements her feet go clack; her legs are as tall as a chimney stack; her fingers flicker like snakes in the air; the walls split open at her green-eyed stare; her voice is as thin as the ghosts of bees; she will crumble your bones, she will make your blood freeze.

Spin a coin, spin a coin,
All fall down;
Queen Nefertiti
Stalks through the town.

Anonymous

2 The poem below has been printed with only the *first* verse as the poet intended it to be. This shows you the pattern of the poem, which will help you with your task.

The rest of the poem has been printed in pairs of lines, but the pairs are not in the right order. Put them into an order which seems to you to make sense. Use as many clues as you can: meaning, punctuation and rhyme are all important.

Write down on a sheet of paper what you decide.

MIXED BREWS

There was once a witch
Who lived in a ditch
And brewed her brews in the hedges.
She gathered some dank
From the deepest bank
And some from around the edges.

1 With a long grey beard,
   Too old to report for duty!

2 And muttering words and curses;
   And every spell

3 Not long since,
   When she wanted a prince

4 Would have worked out well
   If she hadn't mixed the verses.

5 From his uncle cruel and cranky,
   She concocted a spell

6 With a postman's bag
   And threepence to pay on the parcel.

7 With a magic bean
   She called for a Queen

8 To wake the sleeping beauty
   A man appeared

9 She returns to school
   And tries to improve her spelling.

10 What comes of a witch
    Who has hitch after hitch?

11 When she hoped to save
    Aladdin's Cave

12 She practised her charms
    By waving her arms

13 Who was locked in the wizard's castle.
    There came an old hag

14 I'm afraid that there's no telling:
    But I think as a rule

15 That somehow fell
    Not on him but on Widow Twanky.

                              Clive Sampsom

3 The first verse of the poem below is printed in full so that you can see what its pattern is. After that, most of the *verbs* have been taken out of the verses. This is shown by the nine blank spaces.

Work out a set of verbs that you think will fit into the blanks. As well as the meaning, pay attention to the sound of the words, the rhythm of the lines, and the rhymes.

Write down on a sheet of paper the nine verbs you choose. (Each space has only *one* word.)

THE WITCH'S CAT

'My magic is dead,' said the witch. 'I'm astounded
That people can fly to the moon and around it.
It used to be mine and the cat's till they found it.
My broomstick is draughty, I snivel with cold
As I ride to the stars, I'm painfully old,
    And so is my cat;
    But planet-and-space-ship
    Rocket or race-ship
Never shall part me from that.'

She _____ an advertisement, 'Witch in a fix
Willing to part with the whole bag of tricks
_____ cheap at the price of eighteen and six.'
But no one _____ ready to open his coffers
For out-of-date rubbish. There _____ any offers –
    Except for the cat.
    'But planet-and-space-ship,
    Rocket or race-ship
  Never shall part me from that.'

The tears _____ fast, not a sentence she spoke
As she _____ on her broom and the brittle stick _____
Then clean disappeared, _____ no prints;
And no one at all _____ set eyes on her since
    Or her tired old cat.
    'But planet-or-space-ship,
    Rocket or race-ship
  Never shall part me from that.'

Ian Serraillier

In a group

When you and your partner have finished, join up with another pair. Taking
1, 2 and 3 in turn, explain what you decided and *why*. See whether the
other pair had the same ideas as you.

Your own writing

What you do Write about one of the subjects below. They are all connected in some way with witchcraft.

Why? To put into practice some of the things you have learned about using words in this Unit.

To choose a *form* which is well-suited to the subject of your writing.

How? **On your own**

Ideas for writing

1 Write and decorate a witch's recipe for a disaster.

This could look like a recipe taken from a cookery book, or it could be a rhyming chant. It could be menacing or revolting.

2 Write a story showing how a witch tries to prove she is still important in the twentieth century.

This could be written from the point of view of the witch, or someone else, or with the storyteller as an observer. It could be serious or funny. Perhaps the people around don't, at first, realize what is going on, or don't believe . . . .

3 Write a story in which someone suffers a terrible fate for not doing what a witch wants her or him to.

This could also be written from several points of view. The story could be told in the form of a poem, or a series of letters which gradually build up to a climax.

4 Imagine that the things in a house have been bewitched – they no longer do what they are supposed to. Write a story around this idea.

What would happen if the kettle in your house refused to boil, or the vacuum cleaner started to blow rather than suck, or if water came out of the taps only when you switched the light on? Imagine trying to explain why you were late for school, or to people who called to do repairs – especially if they could find nothing wrong.

5 Write the story of a combat through magic between two witches.

You could write this as a round-by-round commentary, as in a boxing or wrestling match.

6 Continue Roland's story from Activity 2 (pages 45–46).

Summing it up

INTERCITY SAVERS

Savers are great value for longer-distance journeys, as you will see from the prices shown. These bargains are available on all Saturday and Sunday trains and on most Monday to Friday trains – see overleaf for details.

● TRAVEL OUT ON THE DATE SHOWN ON YOUR TICKET (No break of journey is allowed on your outward journey)
● RETURN WITHIN ONE CALENDAR MONTH (SAME DAY IF YOU WISH)

From	LONDON			
	Blue Days	With Railcard	White Days	With Railcard
Newbury	£8.90	£5.90	£8.90	£5.90
Westbury	£19.00	£12.55	£24.00	£15.85
Castle Cary	£21.00	£13.85	£28.00	£18.50
Pewsey	£11.50	£7.60	£14.00	£9.25

THESE THREE CARDS COULD SAVE YOUR LIFE
– OR THE LIFE OF SOMEONE YOU KNOW

THE FACTS ABOUT HEART DISEASE

● Heart disease kills more people each year than respiratory diseases, accidents, injuries or any other cause.

● 44% of all premature deaths ... ed by nearly 140,000 ... 75 di... and circulation.

● 1000 children ...

● Heart disease ... working days are ... and circulatory di...

WHAT YOU ...

TO HELP YOURS ...

● Don't start to s...
● Have your bloo... advice.
● Remain slim – obesity sho...
● Cut down on fatty foods...
● ... ular planned exercis... ...ularly good forms of exe...

Join in th...
– Britai...
Figures taken from official Gove...

USA
Lowest fare from
£249 RETURN
● New York £249
● Florida £288
● California £288
● Denver £288
● Washington £288
● Chicago £288
● Columbus £288
2nd edition brochure out now.
Guaranteed no surcharges.
Bon Voyage
18 Bellevue Road, Southampton.
Hampshire SO1 2AU
☎ (0703) 330332

It's boom time for Britain!

With Railcard
£15.20
£9.55
£6.35
£11.55

With Railcard
22.45
15.85
3.20
7.15

Blue Days	With Railcard	White Days	With Railcard
£14.50	£9.55	£18.00	£11.90
£7.10	£4.70	£9...	

What's On

Headlines

What you do   Read the six newspaper stories on the opposite page and invent your own headlines for them.

Why?   To sum up the main idea of each story in a few words.
   To see how a headline brings out some, but not all, parts of the story that follows it.

How?   **On your own**

Read the six newspaper stories and decide what you think is the main thing in each which will make someone want to read them. Write this down as briefly as possible. Then come up with the best headline you can think of for each story.

In a group

Compare the headlines you have written. Explain to one another:

● what aspect, or aspects, of the story you were trying to bring out

● why you chose the exact words you did.

Try to agree which of the suggestions does its job really well, and why. If there is a story for which no one has got a good headline, try to work out one in your group.

Charged with drunken driving, Mr W.D. Brown of Louisville, Kentucky, denied the offence on the grounds that he was blind and that his dog, Bud, had been in charge of the vehicle.

"I have trained Bud to bark twice for a green light and once for a red. If I am going faster than the cars beside me, Bud raps my knee with his tail – once for too slow, twice for too fast," he said.

Admitting that, although he still believed dogs to be colour blind, Bud was doing fairly well, Patrolman Doug Williwood told the court that the car had been changing lanes every ten seconds.

"That is why I charged him. And Bud is not tall enough to see the highway's white lines."

Intelligencer Journal

"We were alerted at about 6:30 p.m.," said Captain Angus Moon of the Orkney Coastguard. "A group of campers told us that a peculiar and somewhat mournful wailing could be heard at the bottom of Rackwick Cliff.

"Soon after we launched the lifeboat we caught a man with his mouth wide open in the beam of our searchlight. We offered him a trip to safety, but he answered that his name was Mr P.T. Jenkins of Dulwich East, that he was singing a hymn to the setting sun, and that he did not wish to be disturbed."

Aberdeen Press & Journal

Play during the first round of the Cricketers' Cup was interrupted when Mr Simon Hazlitt, batting for the Old Cliftonians against Stow Templars, had to avoid being hit on the head by a 3lb. mackerel dropped by a passing seagull.

The Times

The Hamilton District Council Industrial Tribunal has rejected the claims for unfair dismissal presented by a pair of long serving "Mrs Mops", Margaret McLaren and Janet Cunningham.

After a two-day hearing the tribunal decided that the 12-year dispute between the two lavatory attendants as to whether it was better to steep or rinse lavatory brushes overnight erupted into a brawl during which blows were struck and brushes were waved.

A spokesman for the tribunal said: "Although Mrs McLaren was found in a dishevelled state in a car park, Mrs Cunningham was giving away about 2 stone and 20 years."

Glasgow Herald

Interviewed outside the Chalmette courthouse, Lt. Hiram Whooper of the Louisiana State Police said: "At least 600 children have been entered for the *Cutest Baby on Earth* contest and there must have been about the same number of mothers present.

"When we arrived a group of mothers, some of whom had been waiting six hours to have their child judged, had begun singing *America the Beautiful* to drown out the judges' comments, while another group was booing and shouting things like 'Snotface' and 'Meatball' each time a new contestant reached stage centre.

"Finally, when the principal organiser, Mrs Hilarity Jones from Metairie, came to the microphone, she was pelted with a shower of baby bottles and kiddy crowns. In reply she shouted: 'None of you can have your money back!' and kicked the grand trophy, an 8-foot high dummy, into the audience.

"At this point we made the first of over fifty arrests."

Dallas Morning News

The European light heavyweight championship fight between Graciano Rocchigiani and Alexander Bankhand has been cancelled because Miss Winifred Sonderbond, Mr Rocchigiani's fiancée, beat him up during an argument over who should drive to her sister's wedding.

Daily Telegraph

Blurbs

What you do Read the six 'blurbs' on the opposite page. A blurb is a short description of what a book is about, usually printed on the back cover.

Decide how much the books described appeal to you. Then write some blurbs of your own for books you have enjoyed reading.

Why? To see how much you can tell about a book from its blurb.

To talk about books you like, and write brief summaries of some of them.

How? **With a partner**

Take it in turns to read aloud the six blurbs. Then talk about:

● How the blurb-writers try to make each book sound interesting.

● How much of each book's story you can work out from what is said.

● How far you think you would enjoy each book. You can use a 'star-system' for this – five stars means 'a book I cannot afford to miss', one star means 'a book that sounds as if it would not interest me at all'.

On your own

Choose any books which you have enjoyed reading either recently or some time ago. Not all of them need be books which tell a made-up story; some could be adventures from real life.

Write at least two blurbs to go on the back covers of the books you have chosen. Do not write more than ten lines for each. This means that you may start by writing quite a bit more and then cutting down to the most important and interesting things that are likely to attract readers.

To go with one or more of the blurbs, you might like to make a design for the front cover which would tell more about the book and add to its appeal.

1   Ask any detective and he'll tell you that there is no such thing as the perfect crime. Even the cleverest villain's scheme will contain some flaw which could lead to his or her downfall, providing someone is sharp enough to spot it.

In this book you'll be meeting dozens of villains, each of them carrying out some particularly nasty plan. But in each case the villain makes a mistake and ends up being 'foiled again'. Are you a sharp enough detective to spot the flaws?

2   All the time, the picture of the old lady kept slipping into his mind – he couldn't forget the moment when the Honda had crashed. It was an accident, but it had happened because he hadn't known how to ride the bike properly, a bike that he had stolen, that he had been riding without a licence.

A tense vivid story of a boy desperate to avoid discovery, and unable to share the secret of his guilt.

3   Patsy hates her new London flat and her cruel, lazy stepfather. She'd much rather be back with just her mum in that little house behind the amusement arcade in Margate. Soon her worries start to show in a very embarrassing way. But just when things seem really desperate, a completely unexpected chance of escape presents itself . . .

4   The story of three animals who walked home. There was Luath, a young and gentle labrador, with a red-gold coat and a noble head . . . There was Tao, the hunter, a sleek wheat-coloured Siamese cat . . . There was Bodger, the old half-blind tough Bull Terrier, with a strong sense of humour.

Three animals who walked and ran, and fought and struggled together; who escaped death at almost every step; and who finally came home as though they could never again be parted from the dream of their incredible journey.

5   They're the pits. As boys' football teams go, they don't . . . And when ex-Newcastle player Jossy Blair sees their antics on the pitch he suggests their manager would be better off running a safari park than a football team . . .

However, Tracey Gaunt, the team's bucket girl, doesn't intend watching the Grasshoppers collapse without a fight. And her first task is to persuade Jossy to take them on.

6   Spider of Death . . . Lying bound and gagged in the darkness, Nancy knew the deadly spider was creeping closer. Somewhere in the blackness the hideous creature awaited its prey. At any moment it would strike . . .

ISBN 0 09 173191 7
Printed in Great Britain

School report

What you do Read the end-of-year school report on Susan Thomas, written by her subject teachers, on page 64.

Susan's family is moving to a different part of the country. Because she will have to change schools, Susan's tutor has to send a general report about her work. This is printed on page 65.

Compare the two reports, judging how fair and accurate the general report is in summing up the subject teachers' comments. Then rewrite the general report in the light of what you find.

Why? To look closely at two kinds of summary so that you can spot the similarities and differences between them.

To practise for yourself summarising a lot of information after careful reading and note-making.

How? **In a group**

First, appoint a note-maker. Go through the teachers' report subject by subject. Talk about and note down:

- The parts of the general report which seem to match up with what is said in the subject report.

- Any statements in the general report which seem to contradict what is in the subject report.

- Any things which are said in the subject report that are not in the general report and which you think ought to be.

Next, work from your notes and re-write the general report so that it gives as true a picture of Susan's work as possible. You will need to:

- Reach agreement before you put anything down on paper.

- Make sure that everything you write can be backed up by comments in the subject report.

- Decide how the members of your group are going to share the job of re-writing. For instance, are you all going to agree what each sentence should say and have the same person write it . . . or use another method?

When you have finished, compare what you have written with the reports produced by other groups in your class. Be prepared to explain, if necessary, why you have written what you have.

PINFOLD COMPREHENSIVE SCHOOL

Name: SUSAN THOMAS   Class: 2L   Absences: 16

Subject	Ach	Effort	Teacher's Comments
ENGLISH	A	A	· Susan has worked hard this year. She has a good imagination and writes original and interesting stories. She reads widely and with enjoyment and her spoken English is excellent – well done! MK
MATHS.	D+	D	Susan's work is well below standard. She seems to have given up trying. Her test scores have been increasingly unsatisfactory. If she does not make a more determined effort soon she will have to be moved down to a lower set. She can do better. P.R.S.
SCIENCE	D	C-	Susan shows some interest in practical work but she seems easily distracted when it comes to settling down to learning facts. The end-of-year examination showed she had done very little revision. Homeworks have often been unfinished. M.P.
HISTORY	B+		Susan produced an excellent project on her chosen topic – it was carefully prepared and immaculately presented. She shows a lively interest in all aspects of the subject and works responsibly in group discussions. M.M^cC.
FRENCH	C	D+	Susan is an intelligent pupil who is not working to the best of her ability. Her understanding of the language is quite good, but she does not discipline herself sufficiently to learn vocabulary and grammatical rules. T.R.
ART	B+	B	VERY GOOD! SUSAN'S WORK IS DEVELOPING REALLY WELL. HER DRAWING IS SENSITIVE AND SHE IS NEVER SHORT OF ORIGINAL CREATIVE IDEAS. THE DESIGN WORK SHE HAS DONE AT HOME HAS BEEN ESPECIALLY PLEASING. F.A.
GEOGRAPHY.	C.	C.	Susan has plenty to say in group-work, where her ideas are intelligent and thoughtful. Unfortunately, her notebook shows that she lacks care in writing up her work and that she tends to rush, especially in homework. R.A.V.
GAMES.	B-	D	Susan has a lot of natural ability, but only tries when she feels like it. I'm afraid that she wastes too much time in the company of a group of ill behaved pupils. She seems easily led. It is high time that Susan made a determined effort. V.K.

PINFOLD COMPREHENSIVE SCHOOL

Tutor's general report on:

SUSAN THOMAS

Susan is an intelligent girl who is not making the most of her ability. She should be doing much better in all subjects. She seems to lack the determination to settle down to really hard work, especially when she has to work on her own.

Although she shows enthusiasm in practical subjects, Susan is unable to concentrate for any length of time. In class, she does not take easily to group-work, and tends to distract other pupils. Her homework record is varied — she works quite well at things she enjoys but is too ready to give up when faced with difficulty.

Susan can be described as a bit of a 'dreamer' who does things in her own way, and in her own time. She must learn to apply herself to those aspects of school-work which, though they may interest her less, are necessary for her to succeed in the long run. Unless she is dealt with very firmly by her teachers, there is a danger that Susan will allow herself to drift into failure.

Seeing through someone else's eyes

What you do Read the passage 'Getting a Bashing', which begins on the opposite page. It is about a young boy who is chased and set on by a group of bigger, older boys.

Put yourself in the place of the young boy. Write an account of what happens from his point of view, using all the information in the passage you think you need. Make your account as short as you can without losing any of the important details.

Why? To re-tell part of a story from a different point of view.

To describe the main events in the story as briefly as you can.

How? **With a partner**

Work your way through the passage carefully, bit by bit, making notes about the main events as if you were the young boy. You might begin something like this:

1 A group of bigger boys started fighting me.
2 They threw my cap in a puddle and pushed me in after.
3 I started crying.
4 It was a dark alley.
5 An older boy called Woolcott tried to stop them hitting me.

. . . and so on. Do *not* write out any of the words that are actually spoken in the passage. Sum up the conversations as the young boy might describe them later when telling a friend what happened.

GETTING A BASHING

It was a rainy day in November when I met him first, and about a regiment of them seemed to be bashing him. He was a little dark skinny kid who looked about eight, but I knew he couldn't be because of the school cap. It was our school cap, and we don't take kids under eleven. The cap was in a puddle, and so was this kid. He was down on his knee in it, and that's where they were bashing him.

As far as I could see, he was letting them. He wasn't struggling or yelling or anything. He was just kneeling there sobbing, and doing that pretty quietly.

I said, 'All right, break it up.'

It was dark in the alley and they had to peer at me.

'Get lost,' one of them said, uncertainly.

'Yeah, vanish.'

'Scramaroo.'

They let go of him all the same.

I could see they were younger than me, and smaller, which was all right except one of them had some kind of cosh in his hand, a piece of hosepipe or something.

'I know you!' this one yelled suddenly, just about the same moment I realized I knew him, too. He was a tough young kid with an elder brother who'd made my life a misery at another school. 'You're Woolcott, ain't you? I know where you live, Woolcott. Better shove off if you don't want trouble.'

'Yeah, shove.'

'Buzz off. He's ours.'

I said to the kid, 'Get up.'

'You leave him alone,' the kid with the cosh said. 'He started it. He hit one of us.'

'Yeah, he was throwing things.'

'Were you throwing things?' I said to the kid.

He just shook his head, still sobbing.

'Yes you did, you rotten little liar! He caught Harris, didn't he, Harris?'

'Right here,' Harris said, pointing to his temple. 'I've still got a headache.

I said, 'What did he throw?'

'He threw a ball. He threw it flipping hard, too. We was in the timber yard and he run away before we could see who done it.'

'How do you know it was him, then?'

'He told us,' Harris said triumphantly. 'He come up and laughed and told us right out, didn't he?'

'Yeah.'

'Yeah, right out, he did. He done it last Thursday and he come up just now and said it was him. Laughing, too.'

'I only asked for my ball back,' the kid said.

It was the first time he'd spoken, and I looked at him twice because it was

68

with a foreign accent. 'I saw them playing with it and I came up and apologized and asked for it back. It was only an accident. I didn't mean to hit anybody. It went over the wall by mistake.'

'Yeah, you rotten little liar, you threw it.'

'No, please, I didn't. It's the only ball I've got.'

'The only one you *had . . .*'

I said, 'Give him his ball back.'

'You take a jump.'

'Give him it back, quick.'

They were ganging up round me, and the one with the cosh was fingering it, so I made a quick snatch before he was ready and got it off him.

I said, 'Give him his ball.'

One of them pulled a ball out of his pocket and dropped it on the ground, and the kid picked it up.

'My brother'll murder you,' the kid with the brother said.

'Give him his satchel, too.'

'He'll jump about on you. He'll tear you in little pieces. He'll give you such a crunching –'

I said, 'If those are your bikes jump on them quick.'

Their bikes were leaning up against the alley wall and they got on them and pushed off.

'I wouldn't like to be you,' the kid with the brother said.

He said something else, too, but I didn't catch it. They were all laughing as they rode off.

David Line

On your own

When you have made all your notes, start putting them together into story form. Remember that it is the young boy who is 'writing'. Your first few sentences might be something like:

Last Thursday I was playing in the timber yard with a ball. It accidentally went over the wall and hit an older boy, who was hanging about with some friends, on the head. Today I saw them again and asked for the ball back. They got angry and chased me down a dark alley, threw my cap in a puddle and pushed me in after it.

. . . and so on.

It is a good idea to write out the story you are re-telling in rough draft form first, so that you can change, add and rearrange things before you make your final version. This final version should be paragraphed – think carefully about where the paragraph breaks ought to come.

Eyewitness

What you do Separate the useful information from the useless in the statements of three witnesses to a crime. Then put the most valuable information together into a report.

Why? To practise taking the information you need from a piece of writing.

To work out which pieces of information are most useful to you.

To do so by talking your ideas through with someone else so that you can help each other to sort out what you think.

How? **With a partner**

Look at the map on page 71 of the centre of a small town. This shows where a crime – robbery at a jeweller's – was committed and where three witnesses were at the time.

Read the statements by the witnesses. When you have done this, complete the grid on page 74. The first three entries have been filled in to help you get started. The completed grid will give you a set of notes about the probable facts.

On your own

Using your notes, write a statement of what you know.

70

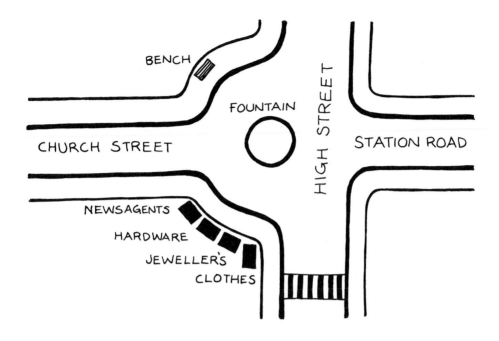

STATEMENTS BY THE THREE WITNESSES

Mrs Maureen Roberts

I was sitting on the bench, you see, taking a break from shopping. Let me see – I was undoing a sweet for our Billy. It was one of his Mickey Mouse ones – they're his favourites you know. Only way to keep him quiet when he gets like that. Big baby! Anyway, what with him whining and the baby crying I couldn't get on with the shopping. Oh, the baby was in his pram. I use that for carrying my bits and pieces in, you see.

Anyway, I suddenly heard this terrible noise. Well, I thought it was one of those bombs going off. I looked up – dropped our Billy's Mickey Mouse – and that set him off even worse. And just across the road – outside the jewellers – there was this big car. Black, I think it was. And I could see two blokes behind it. They were big too – and they had things in their hands. Looked like guns to me. They were getting stuff out of there like nobody's business.

When this bloke came out of the shop and the bloke in the car yelled something and one of the others turned round and bashed this man that came out of the shop. Belted him something wicked, he did. And this poor gentleman fell on the floor and was lying there groaning and bleeding. Terrible, it was. And our baby started crying again because of all the noise. Anyway, the men threw a bag or something in the car and drove off ever so fast. I didn't get the number.

Miss Sharon Kingham

I was just going up to the shops when I noticed this big, old Rover going across the junction in front of me. Dark blue, it was. I used to have a boyfriend who has one just like it. I guess that's why I noticed it. You know how it is. Anyhow, just before I got to the corner I heard a crash. Terrible noise. I thought there must have been an accident. So I ran up to the corner. When I got there – it can only have been a few seconds – I couldn't see any accident. So I looked around to see what was going on. And what I did see was that car – I'm sure it was the same one – an old, dark-blue Rover – parked outside the jewellers. And two fellows with pick-axe handles or something like that were going hammer and tongs at the window. I ran along the High Street without thinking – but when I got to the zebra crossing I stopped. I wasn't getting mixed up with somebody swinging a pick-axe.

I got the car's number, though – ATK 391T. There was one man still in the car. He was the driver. The other two were on the pavement. One was a big fellow – over six foot. The other was shorter – above five foot eight, I should say. The little one was wearing jeans and a sweater – he'd got long hair. The other one looked older – short hair, near enough a crew-cut and going grey. He's the one who hit the shopkeeper when he came running out. It looked to me like he punched him – but I wouldn't swear to it. Anyhow, he went straight out. While that was going on the little one was grabbing stuff from the window and stuffing it in a bag – one of those big green canvas holdalls. Then the big fellow, the older one, yelled something to him and they both dived back into the car. It was disappearing up Church Street before they'd closed the doors. My boyfriend's car never shifted like that.

72

Mrs Mary Chigwell

I was just stepping out of the newsagents when an old Rover stopped outside the jewellers. It must have come fast 'cos the driver really slammed the brakes on. Two men rushed out – they were both carrying pick-axe handles and one of them had a large holdall. They were really frightening, so I went back inside. I called the shopkeeper and she said, 'Get the number while I phone the police'.

She shoved a piece of paper and biro at me and I wrote down the number – BTK 391T. I watched through the window and the two men dropped the bag and started to smash the jeweller's window. The nearest one had his back to me but the other was facing me. The one with his back to me had blue jeans on and a black sweater. He had fair hair – it was straight and came down to his shoulders. I couldn't tell his height because I never saw him standing upright. He looked fairly slim. It only took a few blows to smash the window and then the fair-haired one started grabbing stuff out of the display while the other one seemed to be standing guard. I couldn't see what he was getting out.

The other one was quite big – about six foot and very broad. He had enormous hands. He was wearing an old sports jacket, brown cords and a shirt without a tie. His hair was short and he was bald on top – from the forehead back. He looked about fifty, but it was hard to tell. He had his club in his left hand and when the jeweller came out, he swung round and hit him. The club might have hit the jeweller but I don't think so – it was more of a punch. Then he yelled to the other one to get in the car. The other one said something but the big one grabbed his shoulder and pushed him towards the car. The fair-haired one got in the front, the big one in the back, and the car drove off into Church Street. It was all over in less than a minute.

REPORT SHEET

Enter brief notes on the information you have been able to take from the statements of the three witnesses. If you keep the information in rows across as well as down, leaving a gap where a witness does not say anything, it will be easier to cross-check and decide what is likely to be fact. We have made three entries. Check them – you may not agree that they are right, and even if they are right, you may not feel that they are worth entering.

Report Sheet

Names:			
			Probable
Witness 1	Witness 2	Witness 3	fact.
① Noise	noise	—	
② Big Car. Black?	Big old dark Rover ATK 391T	Old dark blue Rover BTK 391T	Dark blue Rover ?BTK 391T
③ Parked outside Jewellers.	Parked outside Jewellers.	Parked outside Jewellers.	Parked outside Jewellers.
④			

This page may be photocopied

UNIT 6

The world in winter

ACTIVITY 1

A personal anthology

What you do   During the time you are working on this unit, collect your own and/or other people's writing together into an anthology about winter.

Why?   To do a lot of reading and/or your own writing on one subject.
   To choose pieces of writing that you like.
   To work out an order for them.
   To find a way of presenting them so that other people can enjoy them too.

How?   **On your own**

The way you go about doing this will depend on what you decide to do. You may want to do the following:

- Make a collection of other people's writing – so you will need to do a lot of reading.
- Make a collection of your own writing – so you will need to do a lot of writing.
- Mix your own and other people's writing in your collection.
- Collect poems, or extracts from stories, or articles, newspaper reports and other factual accounts. You may decide to stick to only one kind of writing, or to put together lots of different kinds.

Put the items together in the form of:

- a booklet
- *or* a tape
- *or* a wall display.

Illustrate any writing with drawings or photographs. If you make a tape, you might find music helpful.

These are all decisions you need to make. You need to bear in mind:

- what you want to do
- what your audience – the other members of your class and, perhaps, your school – will enjoy.

The way I chose to go

What you do Organize the jumbled-up lines of a poem so that they make sense to you.

Why? To look at the way words can be put together to make most sense and have the strongest effect.

To sort out your own ideas by working with someone else.

How? **With a partner**

The poem on the opposite page is complete. That is, all the words are there and all the lines are there. However, the lines have not been printed in the order the writer intended them to be.

Re-arrange the lines in the order that makes most sense to you. Make use of all the clues you can find. These include the sense of the thing (two or more lines fitting together in some way) and the rhymes.

To help you get started, the first line printed is the original first line.

THE SNOW

1 In no way that I chose to go

2 My footsteps made a shallow space,

3 Snow was my comrade, snow my fate,

4 Could I escape the falling snow.

5 The snow still fell before my eyes.

6 Was on a journey not begun.

7 I shut my eyes, wet with my fears:

8 And then the snow filled up the place,

9 I stopped my ears in deaf disguise:

10 And all the walking I had done

11 The snow still whispered at my ears.

12 In a country huge and desolate.

Clifford Dyment

In a group

When you have put the lines of the poem into an order you and your partner are both happy with, compare your version with that of another pair.

Explain what you have done and why. Listen to what the other pair have to say.

Look particularly at any differences in your versions and try to understand why they have come about and what effect they have.

November

What you do Set, answer and mark some questions about the passage on the opposite page.

Why? To look carefully at *what* is being described in the passage and *how* it is described.
  To think about how to ask questions clearly.
  To think about which questions it is most useful to ask.

How? **With a partner**

Read the passage on the opposite page carefully. Then discuss it with your partner. Work out a clear picture of what is being described in it and which parts of it you think are most important. Then work out a set of questions about these parts.

  Make sure that the way you word your questions makes their meaning clear.

  When you have worked out all the questions you think you need, swap your set with that of another pair. Talk with your partner to agree answers to the questions you have been set and write down your answers.

  When you have finished this – and the other pair have finished answering your questions – hand over your answers and mark each other's work.

In a group

Finally, go through both sets of questions and answers with the other pair. Explain how you have marked each other's answers. Then try to agree about which were the most useful questions to have asked.

NOVEMBER

The November of that year was bitter. It snowed so hard that it soon stopped being fun and became just a nuisance and then a torment. Tom would refuse to go out. He had built a tunnel for himself, raced around with mittens full of snowballs, made stockpiles at strategic points all the way up Church Street; but no one else wanted to play as long or as hard or as often as he did – so he gave up.

His mother seemed to enjoy it. Her post-round took twice as long, but she came back, blazing-fresh, with white petals of snow gleaming and melting in her black, tossed hair, and, if he were lucky, she would tell him of some fight she had had with a particular drift or a lane or a field.

He was invited by his Uncle Henry to go and build a snowman for Catherine – his younger cousin – but he refused to go. His father – who took the bad weather badly and coughed a great deal – was angry with him for this.

Tom went to sleep, shivering, and woke up with his fingers and toes stiff with cold.

The snow battened down the town, snuffing out any flicker of resistance with a heavy fall of thick flakes. People walked silently along white-carpeted streets, or sloshed quickly through brown, running mud.

The north wind began to rise – to rise until it blew down the streets like a great mountain draught. The snow covered itself with ice; the mud stiffened into glass pools. No one had ever known such a wind; it hurled out November and blasted, icily, into the last month of the year as if it were determined to freeze and wither the whole winter. Coats were piled on coats; gloves doubled; socks knitted thick and uncomfortable. But the wind cut through everything.

His mother told Tom to go out and walk himself warm. To stump through the fields in his wellingtons until he sweated so much that he would not mind taking off all his clothes and rolling over and over on the crackling top of the deep snow. She sometimes felt like doing that herself, she said.

He would not go out. Sitting inside the house, he looked out at the slate sky and the slate-coloured houses. Anything that stirred was out of place.

Melvyn Bragg

Just suppose

What you do Suppose winter were not just something which came and went, but something which came and stayed and stayed and stayed. Suppose snowfall and ice lasted for three or four months.

It would be very different from the normal winter — but what might it be like? Write a story to get across your ideas about this, following the instructions on the opposite page.

Why? To use what you know about a normal winter to work out what an extreme one might be like.

To work out the background for a story.

How? **In a group**

As a group, talk about all the problems you think a long, very severe winter might cause. Make a note of each of these problems down one side of a sheet of paper, leaving several lines between each entry. Here is an example:

Problem	Probable effects on people
Blocked roads	difficult/impossible to get to: work school the shops hospital etc.
Power cuts	no light or heat at times cooking difficult
No telephone	

You already know the difficulties which really bad winter weather can create. Talk about how much worse it could be. Put down as many different ways in which people could be affected.

When you have made your list, talk about what could be done to overcome the problems and what you think would actually happen. (What could be done and what would happen are not necessarily the same.)

You now have the background information to write a story. Imagine one or two people trying to live in the world which you have been talking about. Write his, her or their story.

Your own writing

What you do Write in one of several ways to put your ideas about the world in winter into words of your own.

Why? To explore your own ideas about winter more fully.
   To put into practice some of the things about writing that you have learned from earlier work.

How? **On your own**

Choose one of the following topics and decide how you want to write about it.

Ideas for writing

1 Write a poem or prose piece about a memory of winter that is particularly vivid to you.

2 Write a story set in winter – base it on your own experience *or* make something up *or* use a mixture of the two.

3 Write a description of a place that you know well in the depths of winter – try to capture the mood as well as the appearance of winter.

4 Write a poem or prose piece showing winter from two points of view.

5 Use the title 'The First Snowfall of Winter' in any way that appeals to you.

The way you say it

85

Fill-in-a-script

What you do　On the opposite page is the 'script' of a conversation between a teacher and a pupil. All the things which the pupil says have been left out.

　　Your task is to fill in the gaps by writing down what you think the pupil says.

Why?　To work out from various clues what has been left out of a passage of conversation.

　　To write in the 'missing links' so that the whole conversation makes sense and sounds realistic.

How?　**On your own**

Read through the passage, skimming over the gaps. You will begin to work out what the pupil might be saying as you look at the teacher's remarks before *and* after each gap.

　　On a sheet of paper, write down your ideas for what the pupil says each time he/she speaks. Use the numbers printed by each gap to do this.

Try to make the conversation as realistic as you can.

● What would a pupil of your age really say?

● What tone of voice would he/she use?

● What would the pupil be feeling like, and how would this be shown in the way he/she speaks?

How much you write in each gap is up to you. Be careful not to make the pupil's remarks too short – write as much as you like, providing the whole conversation makes sense when you have finished.

With a partner

Read aloud your completed script. Your partner acts as the teacher when your script is being read, then you do the same for theirs.

　　Talk about what differences there are between the two conversations. Give your opinion about how 'real' they sound.

'MISSING HOMEWORK'

The scene is any classroom in any school. The teacher (A) is going round a second-year class, collecting in last night's homework. He has got as far as his least favourite pupil (B).

A: Right. Where's your homework, then?

B: .... (1)

A: Come on, come on, I wasn't born yesterday. I've heard *that* excuse before.

B: .... (2)

A: Heaven help us! Now I *have* heard everything. What's the dog got to do with it?

B: .... (3)

A: Oh, so you did *try* to stop it, then?

B: .... (4)

A: Yes, a very likely story! And I suppose it never occurred to you to ask your mother to write a note explaining all this, did it?

B: .... (5)

A: Oh, she *did*, did she? Well, come on, I'm waiting. Hand it over.

B: .... (6)

A: You really are accident-prone, aren't you?

B: .... (7)

A: Well, in that case I think you'd better come up here after school today and do it then. In your own time.

B: .... (8)

A: That will just have to wait, won't it?

B: .... (9)

A: No more excuses – I've heard quite enough, thank you. After school today, remember. And you'd better make sure to be prompt. (*A walks away.*)

B: .... (10)

(The scene ends)

Put it this way...

What you do Write, and then read aloud, three conversations involving the same person – a second-year pupil. The events which give rise to the conversations are as follows:

There has been some trouble on the school premises during morning break. Three second-years are playing with a tennis ball. The ball hits an older pupil on the back of the head. After some shouting, a scuffle breaks out and one of the second-year pupils ends up on the floor. The older brother of this pupil (a fifth-year) comes along and a fight develops. Finally, a teacher, the Head of Second Year, breaks it up. There is some discussion in the Year Head's Office. Following this, the second-year pupil is sent home.

The conversations for you to write are between:

1 The second-year pupil and the Year Head in the office.

2 The second-year pupil and his/her mother when the pupil arrives home unexpectedly during the morning.

3 The second-year pupil and a friend who was involved in the incident, on the way to school next morning.

Why? To show through your writing that how you speak, as well as what you say, depends on whom you are talking to.
To practise telling a story entirely through speech.

How? **On your own**

You are the pupil at the centre of the 'trouble'. In order to make the conversations true-to-life, think hard about the three people you speak to.

- How will each of them be feeling towards you?

- How will they differ in the way they feel?

- How will this affect the way they speak?

Equally important, how will you speak to each of them?

- How will you feel in the Year Head's office?

- How will you feel when you arrive home during the morning?

- Will you give different versions of what happened to each person (or put the emphasis on different things)?

With a partner

Read your conversations aloud. You read what the pupil says; your partner reads what the other three people say. Talk about the differences and similarities in what you have written. How realistic do you each think the other's conversations are? Why?

Scenes for a play

What you do Read the story 'Lian and the Magic Brush'. Take two of the most dramatic parts of the story and write them out as scenes for a play.

Why? To put into practice what you have learned about how conversations can be used to tell a story, to show people's characters and to bring out feelings.

  To work with others to produce a play-script which can be read aloud, and/or taped, and/or acted out.

How? **In a group** (The ideal number for this Activity is four.)

Read the story. The passages marked 1 and 2 are the parts you will change into play form.

  Read passages 1 and 2 again, very carefully. Then, before you write down anything at all, talk about the following things to do with passage 1.

- How many characters apart from Lian and the landlord are you going to have speaking?

- What kind of man is the landlord? What are the best ways of bringing out his character?

- In the middle paragraph of passage 1, no one speaks, according to the way the story is written. How are you going to get across what happens in this part when you change it to play form?

- Are you going to use any stage-directions? (A stage direction tells the actors how to speak, how to move and what actions to perform.) If so, where?

- What is going to be the climax of this scene? Is it going to be funny or sad?

Ask similar questions of your own about passage 2.

  Now divide your group up, so that two people work on the first scene and two on the second. Make a rough draft of your scene, putting the names of the characters in capital letters on the left and any stage directions in brackets. You will need a lot of 'rough' paper — as you work, you will probably find yourselves adding and changing bits until your scene sounds right.

Come back together as a group. Each pair should read aloud the scene they have been working on, playing all the parts! Say what you think of each other's scenes, making any changes you all agree are needed. Then write the scenes up in their 'best' form. Finally, either tape or act out your scenes. (If you wish, you could go on to make up 'The Further Adventures of Lian'.)

LIAN AND THE MAGIC BRUSH

In a small village in China there once lived a boy whose name was Han Ma Lian. The Chinese put their personal name last, and so he was known to everyone as Lian. When he was small, both his parents died, and he had to earn his living for himself by cutting wood in winter and weeding the fields in summer. He worked hard, but the money he earned was only just enough to live on with none to spare. This made Lian sad, because his great wish was to learn to paint and he could not even afford to buy himself a paint-brush.

One day he was walking through the nearby town when he saw a teacher painting a picture in a private school. Scarcely thinking what he was doing, Lian walked inside and asked the teacher if he would give him a brush, as he wanted to paint so much. The schoolmaster looked at him in astonishment, Lian being just like a bundle of old rags. He boxed Lian's ears after telling him that the great art of painting was not meant for beggars. Lian protested that he was not a beggar, but the schoolmaster would hear no more and turned him out of the school. He took up his brush again and tried to forget about being interrupted, leaving Lian to walk unhappily away.

However, Lian did not give up hope. If he could not work with the correct materials, he would practise with whatever came to hand. After a long day on the mountain-side gathering great bundles of sticks, he would set down his burden for a while and look for a flat rock. On it he would draw pictures with a sharp stone – landscapes, beasts and birds. When he went down to the river to fish, he would spend the last hour tracing outlines in the sun-baked mud with a sharp stick. At home he covered the walls of his cave with drawings of the things he had seen during the day, so that the other villagers would stare in surprise and say the pictures seemed to be alive, they were so full of expression. Lian was held back by only one thing – he still needed a brush.

One night, as he lay asleep in his cave, he dreamt that a very old man approached his bed. In his hand was a paint-brush with a handle of gold, and this he held out to Lian. 'Take it,' he said. 'You have the power in your hands to make good use of it. Be careful, though, because it has unusual powers.' The old man placed the brush on the end of the bed and went out of Lian's cave.

When Lian woke up the next morning, he sighed deeply at the memory of his dream. Sadly, he got up to do his day's work, and as he did so a golden paint-brush rolled onto the floor. Lian realised with delight that his 'dream' had really happened. Now he could paint like an artist! The first picture he made was of a bird in flight. As he completed the last feather on its wing, the bird rose up from the paper and flew out of the cave, making a sigh like the wind. When his first astonishment was over, Lian painted a fish. As soon as he had finished, it lay gasping on the paper, and he ran outside to throw it in the stream. All day he painted with his magic brush, and every object he drew turned into something alive.

From that day on, Lian weeded no more fields and collected no more firewood. Instead he used his power to help the whole village. If a poor peasant needed a plough but could not afford one, Lian drew one for him. If an old widow wanted a new oil lamp to see her way in winter, she came to Lian and he was happy to paint one of the finest quality. If a young couple were just married, they would make a list of the things they needed, like chairs and tables, and Lian was happy to produce them with great skill.

1 His fame spread throughout the village, and the local landlord, who was mean and greedy, sent for Lian to come and work in his home. Lian, however, refused politely, for he had no wish to help make the rich landlord any richer. The next day, two tough-looking servants appeared outside Lian's cave and forced him to go with them to the landlord's house, where he was locked in the stables until he decided to co-operate. The landlord ordered Lian to do as he wished, but Lian refused; then the landlord offered him bribes; then, while he still refused, the landlord made threats and stormed out, leaving Lian locked in the stables.

As it was the middle of winter, and snow lay on the ground, the landlord thought that a couple of days of cold and hunger would be enough to make Lian see that he had better change his mind. On the second evening, he dressed himself in his furs and went over to the stables. He was surprised to see a reddish glow coming from inside through a chink in the door. He peeped in and saw Lian sitting comfortably beside a blazing stove, with a plate of rice and fish and a bowl of wine beside him on a little table. He had painted all the things he needed to make himself comfortable.

The landlord was furious. He ran back to the house and ordered his servants to bind Lian with ropes, but when they opened the stable door they found that the boy had drawn a rope ladder and escaped up it. The landlord tried to follow but he fell off: Lian had been rushed into making the ladder and the rungs were not firm enough to bear the landlord's great weight. He ordered the horses to be saddled and set off in chase of Lian with some of his men, but Lian saw them coming and drew a bow and arrow with which he shot the landlord through the chest. While his servants gathered anxiously around the wounded man, Lian drew a mighty horse and used it to make his escape.

Lian dared not return to the village for the time being. Instead, he went from one town to another, making his pictures and selling them in order to earn his living. He was careful, though, never to complete a painting, leaving out some tiny detail from each, because he did not want to find himself in more trouble from the power of his wonderful brush.

2 One day he was working in a big city when someone accidentally jogged his arm and a spot of paint fell just where the eye should have been in a hawk that he was painting. This was the detail that Lian had purposely left out, and the bird now rose up above the market-place, to the astonishment of all who saw it. They murmured their amazement, and someone ran off to tell the Emperor, who commanded Lian to present himself at the palace without delay. Unwillingly he went. The Emperor ordered him to paint a dragon, but Lian saw that this man was the same sort as the landlord, and he pretended to have misunderstood. He painted a toad instead, which made the courtiers feel sick and the Emperor annoyed.

As a punishment, Lian was again put in prison, but this time his brush was taken from him and he was helpless. The Emperor, a greedy man, took the brush and painted a mountain of gold. When it was done, he was not satisfied and painted six more, piling them so high on top of each other that they toppled over, almost crushing him to death. Then he changed his tactics and painted gold bricks instead. Each one was bigger than the last until he finally made one that was as long as a broomstick. He held it lovingly, but in a flash it changed into a python and hissed angrily. Only the Emperor's armed guards saved him from a terrible death.

He realised he could not do without Lian's help. The boy was released from prison and brought back to the palace, where the Emperor offered him a princess to marry if only he would paint what was asked of him. Lian did not want to marry the princess, but he pretended to agree and the Emperor told him to paint the ocean. The Emperor asked for some fish to go in the sea and Lian agreed, and dolphins could be seen cutting the surface of the water, while flying-fish skimmed above the waves. Next, the greedy Emperor ordered a handsome boat to go sailing in, and Lian produced one, adding a gang-plank so that everyone in the Emperor's court could walk on board.

Soon everyone except Lian was on board the boat. After they had pulled the ropes and stamped on the deck planks to make sure they were real, the Emperor and his courtiers were ready for adventure. Lian was told to make the wind blow to fill the sails. He painted little clouds, and made the sails billow out. He painted more and bigger clouds, until the ship was racing along, and then he made the waves rise higher and higher, until the Emperor was soaked to the skin and clinging to the mast. Lian went on painting waves until at last they swept over the ship and it sank to the ocean bed. Everyone on the ship, of course, was drowned.

Lian took up his brush and went away. What happened to him after that no one knows for certain. Some say he wandered all over China, helping the poor wherever he went to get whatever they most needed. Others say that he returned to his own village, and lived in peace for the rest of his days.

Phillip Payne

UNIT 8

Frights
and fears

ACTIVITY 1

How will it work out in the end?

What you do Read the story below part by part and try to work out what you think is going to happen next.

Why? To think about·one way in which a story can be put together.

    To work out how a story may go by using your own experience of similar stories.

    To explain and, if necessary, defend your ideas.

How? **In a group**

Read the first part of the story, then try to agree answers to the questions which follow it. Do not go on to the second part until you are told to do so.

    (There are 11 parts to this story, all of which are quite short. Cover over the parts you still have to read as you work your way through the story.)

1 George Bunnage leant forward into the wind. His right hand eased the throttle backward and the Yamaha burst forward at seventy-five miles an hour. The dawn autumnal mist seemed to part before the straight beam of his headlight. Deep-cut tyres bit into the wet road. Inside his leathers George was warm and secure: outside, a cold nip in the rushing air worried at the visor of his helmet and sent a chill round his forehead.

    Only four miles to go.

1 What do you think is going to happen next in this story?
2 What do you think might happen in the story as a whole?
3 What time of year is it? What time of day? How might these things be important?
4 What does the last sentence suggest to you?

2 His mind cast back to the last time he had travelled this road. Exactly a year ago. The same time: the same speed. The same houses, shops, trees; the same turnings, junctions; the same traffic lights. Even, it seemed, the same traffic coming the other way. But surely not the same ending to the

journey? Why was he traversing this road again? As the Yamaha urged itself
forward, George racked his brains but found no answer.

1 Have you changed your mind about anything now? What new or
  different ideas have you got? Give reasons for your answer.
2 The word 'same' is repeated over and over again in this part of the story.
  Can you suggest reasons to explain this?

3 He remembered it all. A party till the small hours: then a breakneck
ride home. Forty miles to go. In half-an hour at that time of night? No
trouble. Roaring, bucketing along, master of the smooth motor underneath
him. King of the road, he had exulted to himself. I'm king of the road.

But was he now? Though he continued to rack his brains, he just did not
know any more. His tight-fitting riding leathers seemed to grip tighter round
his waist as he leant into a right-hand bend.

1 What have you now learnt about the last time he made this journey?
2 What are the differences between the way he felt then and the way he
  feels now?
3 Have you changed your ideas about what might happen in the story?
  Explain why they are the same or different.

4 Yes, that night a year ago had been one to remember. If only he could
remember it: if only the question that over-rode everything else would
not keep surging into his mind. Well, that was partly why he was travelling
this road again. But what good could he do?

George braked as he approached a turning to the left: as the Yamaha
slowed, suddenly the grip round his waist tightened and he seemed to be
pulled ever so slightly backwards.

1 Why do you think the writer chose not to let George remember the
  journey a year ago?
2 In the last sentence we are told for the second time about something
  pulling at his waist. What might it be? What new ideas does this give
  you?

5 Two miles to go. The mists were rising: the day would be fine. A year
ago, they were closing in for a dull, dark day. Perhaps that was why
it happened. George's mind was so confused that he could not tell any more.
There seemed to be some sort of weight on his left shoulder; the grip round
his waist was even tighter. He felt very conscious of his own body. The
thought crossed his mind that he might be sickening for something.

1 What idea does the first sentence give you?
2 The idea of weight, of something pulling at him comes in again. Do you believe he might be ill? If not, what do you believe?

6 A mile. Half a mile. A car parked by the road just ahead. Pull out to pass it. Look in the mirror first.

George caught his breath. In the mirror: what was it? A view back up the deserted road – yes. But what else? What was behind him? What shadow seemed to be over his shoulder? A trick of light as the sun began to rise?

It must be. The whole affair was ludicrous. Nothing had happened last year in the next quarter of a mile. It had all been his imagination, and the urge to retrace his steps a year later was absolute lunacy.

1 The distance is getting shorter. Why might the writer want to keep telling you this?
2 The second paragraph is full of questions. Why do you think the writer has asked the questions but not answered them?
3 What do you think the answers to those questions might be?

7 Very close now. Soon he would see the lights of that pedestrian crossing, deserted at night but still sending out its meaningless message with no one to heed it – red, green, flashing amber. No one to heed it in the early morning – so who cares if the light is red? Straight through it: don't slacken speed.

All right on a bright morning like this. Nearly all right on a dark, dark dawn with the fog coming. Chances are always worth taking when you think you can get away with them.

1 What has the writer now told you that he has been holding back? Why has he told you now?
2 What do you now think is going to happen?

8 This morning, as they came into view, they were red. Just like last time. But now it was all clear, all deserted.

So, thought George, I'll pull the throttle back, roar through the lights at eighty and show myself that last year everything was all right.

The grip round his waist, the weight on his shoulder, were stronger than ever. Even as his fingers started tuning the throttle he had an urge to look behind him. He fought it. The Yamaha leapt forward.

1 What do you think George is trying to prove to himself?
2 What is different between this time and the last time?
3 Why do you think he wants to look behind? If he did, what might he see?

98

9 Last year it had been different. Now it came back clearly. Last year he had carried on through the lights, had too late seen a shape step off the pavement, had felt the shock of collision, fought to keep control, righted himself and roared away without looking back, leaving a huddled, bleeding bundle on the road for others to pick up later.

Without looking back. But now, a year later, the urge to look back was too great.

1 What happened last year? Is this what you expected?
2 There are still two parts of the story to go. If George looks back this time, what do you think he will see?

10 Only a snatched, split second look as he turned his head. But what he saw was burned in his mind for the instant he had left to live. To his right he looked, straight into burning eyes set in a skull behind a helmet resting, weighing down on his shoulder. And he felt the grip of bony hands inside the gauntlets grip harder into his waist and an inexorable pull from behind. And he seemed to see a huddled bundle rise from the road behind him and a standing figure smiling with satisfaction.

1 George does look back; what does he see?
2 What does the last sentence suggest to you?

11 At the inquest a verdict of 'misadventure' was passed. The deceased had lost control of his vehicle on the wet road: no blame could be attached to anyone. The coroner drew attention to the fact that two fatalities had occurred in the vicinity over the year before. Perhaps it could be classed as an accident 'black spot', though what hidden dangers could lurk in so innocent a stretch of suburban road quite defeated him.

1 What do we know that the coroner did not know?
2 What do you make of the last sentence?
3 What do you think would be a suitable title for this story?

Dennis Hamley

Nightmare

What you do Read Michael Rosen's poem, 'Nightmare'. Work out from reading the beginning of the poem how you think the end of it should be set out.

Why? To look carefully at how the lines of a poem can be arranged to create an effect.

How? **With a partner**

This poem has been set out in twelve sections, like paragraphs. Sections 1 to 8 are printed as the poet wanted them. Sections 9 to 12 contain all the words he used, but the lines are not arranged as he wanted them.

Talk about the way Michael Rosen has organized the lines in sections 1 to 8. Use what you learn from this to help you make sense of the rest of the poem.

Then arrange the lines of sections 9 to 12 in the way you think creates most strongly the 'nightmare' effect the poet wanted.

NIGHTMARE

1   I'm down
   I'm underground

2   I'm down the Underground

3   Waiting

4   Waiting for a train

5   There's the platform
   There's the lines
   There's the tunnel
   There's the lines.

6   I'll wait down there
   Down between the lines
   Waiting for the train
   Down between the lines
   and wait for the train
      down there.

7   Look

8   Look up the tunnel look
   Yes
   It's coming, it's coming they say
   And it is
   And I'm between the lines
   And I can see it
   See it coming
   And I'm between the lines

9   Can't someone give me a hand up? Can't you see? I'm between the lines
   and the train's coming give me a hand someone give me a hand the
   train's coming give me a hand I can't climb up the train's coming and
   the platform's sliding in towards me too with the train still coming
   coming down the tunnel the platforms sliding sliding in towards
   me too.

10 I'm still down
   Can't anyone see me down between the lines?

11 Look see me the train platform me the train near now nearer now nearer
   and nearer now NOW

12 That's all.

Michael Rosen

Posting letters

What you do Read the poem 'Posting Letters' by Gregory Harrison.
Talk about the way a poet uses words to create a particular atmosphere in a poem.

Why? To see how words, and patterns of words, can be used to create a strong atmosphere.
To help you in your own writing and in reading other poems and stories.

How? **With a partner**

Read through the poem together to get a general idea of what it is about.
Make two lists. The first list should include all the words and phrases that tell you about the movements of the girl or boy who is 'talking' in the poem and the things around him/her.
The second list should include all the words and phrases that describe or suggest sounds and silence.

In a group

Join another pair. Compare your lists.

Talk about:

- The reasons you think the writer had for choosing the words and phrases in your lists which particularly interest you.

- The parts of the poem you like best and those you like least. Can you explain why? Do you all agree?

102

POSTING LETTERS

There are no lamps in our village,
And when the owl-and-bat black night
Creeps up low fields
And sidles along the manor walls
I walk quickly.
    It is winter;
The letters patter from my hand
Into the tin box in the cottage wall;
The gate taps behind me,
And the road in the sliver of moonlight
Gleams greasily
Where the tractors have stood.
    I have to go under the spread fingers of the trees
Under the dark window of the old man's house,
Where the panes in peeling frames
Flash like spectacles
As I tip-toe.
But there is no sound of him in his one room
In the Queen Anne shell,
Behind the shutters.

I run past the gates,
Their iron feet gaitered with grass,
Into the church porch,
Perhaps for sanctuary,
Standing, hand on the cold door ring,
While above
The tongue-tip of the clock
Clops
Against the hard palate of the tower.
    The door groans as I push
And
Dare myself to dash
Along the flagstones to the great brass bird,
To put one shrinking hand
Upon the gritty lid
Of Black Tom's tomb.
    Don't tempt whatever spirits stir
In this damp corner,
But
Race down the aisle,
Blunder past font,
Fumble the door,
Leap step,
Clang iron gate,
And patter through the short-cut muddy lane.

Oh, what a pumping of breath
And choking throat
For three letters.
And now there are the cattle
Stirring in the straw
So close
I can hear their soft muzzling and coughs;
And there are the bungalows,
And the steel-blue miming of the little screen;
And our own knocker
Clicking like an old friend;
And
I am home.

Gregory Harrison

Your own writing

What you do Choose from the topics below a piece of writing about something frightening. It can be real or imagined, either a poem or a story.

Why? To put into practice some of the things about writing that you have spent most of this Unit talking about.

In particular, to work with your own ideas to create a sense of atmosphere.

How? **On your own**

Choose one of the following topics and write about it in whatever way you find best.

Ideas for writing

1 Invent – or remember – a nightmare.

2 Write about a time when you had to do – or made yourself do – something which absolutely terrified you. Try to include as much detail as possible.

3 The church in activity 3 in this section (page 103) is an important part of the setting in which the action happens. Think of a place which frightens you or which frightened you when you were younger and use it as the setting for a story or poem.

4 It is late at night. Your parents are out. You are alone in the house. You hear a tapping at the window. What is it? What happens?

Assessing writing

ACTIVITY 1

What is important in writing?

What you do Talk about what it is important to be able to do in order to write well.

Why? To get a clear idea of what it means to write well.

To be able to take an active part in judging your own writing.

To see what you need to do to get better at writing.

How? **On your own**

Printed on the opposite page is a list of some of the things you may think are important about writing.

Read through the list – or that part of it the class is working on – and decide which points you agree with and which you do not.

Then decide which you think are the most important points. Tear a sheet of paper into eight parts and write one important point on each piece.

If there are any other things which you think are important but which are not on the list, make a note of those too.

In a group

Write the words 'What you need to do to be a good writer' on a sheet of paper and place it in the middle of the table around which you are working.

Go through the list on the opposite page, taking each of the points in order.

If you have written the point down, put your piece of paper on the table. Put it near to the sheet in the middle if you strongly agree; if it is not that important to you, put it further away. If you do not think it is important at all, you will not have a piece of paper to put down.

Each member of the group should keep a note of what has been agreed and of any points about which there was a lot of disagreement.

Now take it in turns to explain what you think, and talk about your different opinions. When you have said everything that needs to be said, go on to the next point. Continue this until you have worked through all of the list that you were working with.

Finally, talk about any other points which any member of the group thinks are important when judging writing.

Report your conclusions to the rest of the class and try to build up a single class list.

To do any kind of writing well you need to:

1 spell properly

2 punctuate clearly

3 use paragraphs

4 write sentences that are not all the same

5 choose words carefully.

To write stories well you need to:

6 think of and build up interesting situations

7 think of and build up interesting characters

8 think of and build up interesting places

9 use your imagination

10 use your memory

11 organize the story so it makes sense

12 organize different stories in different ways

13 draw attention to the most important things

14 pick out the right details when you describe things

15 write different kinds of stories, not the same kind all the time.

To put your opinion across clearly you need to:

16 think out clearly what you want to say

17 explain what you think and why you think it

18 show the evidence that proves your point

19 reach a conclusion based on your argument

20 keep to the point and not get sidetracked.

Making use of the checklist

What you do Use the list of things that are important about writing, which your group or class has made, to look at some examples of your own work.

Why? To see how well the list works.
  To see how useful it is.
  To get a clearer idea of what you are good at and what things you need to pay more attention to in your writing.

How? **On your own**

The list you have made will help you to see what is important in your writing. However, writing is not a matter of being able to do something or not do it. Some things a person is just beginning to do, others they are getting better at, others he/she can already do well.

To help you see how well you are doing, make out a form or use a photocopy of the one on the opposite page, writing into the boxes the list of things you have agreed.

On your own

Read through two or three recent pieces of your own writing.

Mark off on the list you have made:

- those things you think you are good at
- those things you think you are not good at but are getting better at
- those things you think you have made a start at, but cannot do very well yet

Do not show your results to your partner yet.
  Now swap the pieces of writing you have been reading through and do the same thing for your partner's work.

With a partner

When you have done this, talk to each other about how you see your own and your partner's writing.

MY WRITING

I am:			Your group or class list goes here
starting	getting better at	good at	

Signed .... Date ....

Snapshots, shape poems and Haiku

十九日

二百ナリ

狸ノ戸ニ オトツル、ハ尾ヲモテ扨クト

人ヲメルト尤ニハアラス戸ニ背ヲキツクル

音ナリ

秋の夜は化る狸うる子

引いをとらひ毎や

Completing the picture

What you do Work out which line fits which space in each of eight short poems. Then give each poem a title.

Why? To work with a group of short poems and see how each gives a short 'snapshot' picture of something.
   To show your understanding by working out which line best fits the meaning and pattern of each poem.
   To sum up in a few words what each poem is saying by giving each one a title.

How? **With a partner**

Read through these eight short poems, A – H. One line has been left out of each poem. These lines are printed after all the poems, but not in the right order. You have to work out which line goes into which poem.
   When you have done this, give each poem a short title. This should have no more than two or three words and should sum up what you think the poem is about.

A The winter trees like great sweep's brushes
Poke up from deep earth, black and bare,

....
Of sooty rooks into the air.
                              L.A.G. Strong

B snow crackles underfoot
like powdered bones
trees have dandruff in their hair
and the wind moans
   the wind moans
ponds are wearing glasses
with lenses three feet deep

....
and the wind can't sleep
   the wind can't sleep   *Roger McGough*

113

C
The fog comes
on little cat feet.

. . . .

over harbor and city
on silent haunches
and then moves on.

Carl Sandburg

D
The beach is a quarter of golden fruit,
a soft ripe melon
sliced to a half-moon curve,
having a thick green rind
of jungle growth;

. . . .

with its sharp,
white teeth.

W. Hart-Smith

E
He clasps the crag with hooked hands;
Close to the sun in lonely lands,
Ringed with the azure world he stands.

. . . .

The wrinkled sea beneath him crawls;
And like a thunderbolt he falls.

Lord Tennyson

F
He hangs between his wings outspread
   Level and still
And bends a narrow golden head,
   Scanning the ground to kill.

. . . .

   Round the hill-side,
He looks as though from his own wings
   He hung down crucified.

Andrew Young

114

G Behold the duck.
It does not cluck.
A cluck it lacks.
It quacks.

....

Of a puddle or a pond.
When it dines or sups,
It bottoms ups.

Ogden Nash

H A silver-scaled Dragon with jaws flaming red
Sits at my elbow and toasts my bread.

....

He hands them back when he sees they are done.

William Jay Smith

1   It sits looking

2   I hand him fat slices, and then, one by one,

3   Suddenly stir, and shake a crowd

4   It is especially fond

5   Yet as he sails and smoothly swings

6   He watches from his mountain walls

7   birds are silent in the air

8   and the sea devours it

In a group

Finally, join another pair. Decide which of these short poems you like best and talk about the reasons for your choice.

Making a picture with words

What you do   Write a 'snapshot' poem yourself.

Why?   To express a single idea vividly in a few lines.
                  To choose only those details which are most important.

How?   **On your own**

Remember:

- something which once happened to you
- *or* something which you once saw
- *or* a curious object
- *or* an interesting place
- *or* anything which stands out from the ordinary.

Get a clear picture of it in your mind and think about the things that really matter – get rid of unnecessary detail and clutter. Then write it down in any way you like.

Now form it into a poem.

- Listen to the sound of the words.

- What can you do to make the sound help the meaning?

- Will rhymes help what you want to say or just get in the way?

- Where does it make sense to finish a line and start a new one?

- Would a comparison help anywhere?

- Can you say anything more neatly and in fewer words?

You need to work at this – the more you can say in the fewer words the better.

Patterns of words

What you do Read and discuss the group of 'shape' poems on pages 118–120.

Why? To see how the way words are arranged on the page can be part of the meaning and effect of a poem.

How? **In a group**

Read and talk about these poems. Talk especially about the way the poets have used the shape of the words as part of the effect of the poems.

Try writing out one of the poems without the pattern of words on the page. Is the effect the same? Can you get the same effect in any other way?

Try to see how the words and ideas and shape all fit and work together.

Do you enjoy any one of these poems more than the others? Try to say why. Do the others in your group feel the same as you or differently? What are their reasons?

INVASION

WITH THE FIRST
THE GULLS
EDGE OF LIGHT
CAME BEATING IN
FROM THE SEA
OVER

THE FARMLAND INTO
ROOFCOUNTRY, DUST-
BIN COUNTRY, WAKING THE
TOWN

FROM ITS SUNDAY   MORNING BED THEY
FILLED THE AIR WITH THE
SCREAMS

FILLED THE PALE
OF THEIR DISSENSION,   ARROGANT
SKY WITH THEIR
STRONG

WEAVING THEY BUILT
WINGS, WHEELING AND
A TOWERING PATTERN OF FLIGHT
ABOVE THE
TOWN.

Pamela Gillilan

118

CUP-FINAL

T. O'Day

W.E. March   T.O.G. Lory

J. Usty   O. Uwait   N. See

G. O'Dow

A. Day   W. Ewill   N. Infa   H.I. Story

Young   N. Fast   M. O'Reskill   I.T. Sreally

W. Egot

A.L.L. Sewnup   W.E. Rethel   A.D.S. Whollrun

A. Round   W. Embley

W.I. Thecup

Roger McGough

SKY DAY DREAM

WITH THEM

COULD FLY OFF

I WISHED THAT I

INTO THE SKY

FLY OFF

SOME CROWS

ONCE I SAW

Robert Froman

Making patterns with words

What you do Write some 'shape' poems of your own.

Why? To explore the ways in which a few words, carefully set out, can say something to a reader.

To separate essential from unimportant detail.

To be very disciplined in your choice and arrangement of words.

How? **On your own**

Each of the 'shape' poems you worked with on pages 118–120 presented a clear, sharp picture and used the way the words were set out as part of its meaning. Your task now is to do the same.

To help you get started, try one of the following ideas:

● Think of sounds you particularly dislike – for example, drills, machines, low-flying jets. Try out the ideas the sounds suggest to you.

● Think of different emotions – for example, anger, peacefulness, loneliness, joy. Jot down the words one of these feelings suggest to you and then see how you can shape them and build on them.

● Think of a simple shape – for example, a kite, a football, a wheel, a candle. Rapidly write down all the ideas that shape triggers in your mind and then work them into the shape itself.

● For a few minutes, jot down all the words and phrases that come into your head – try not to think, just let the ideas flow, then look at what you have got and see what you can do with all or part of it.

Reading Haiku

What you do Read a number of Haiku and answer questions about them.

Why? To introduce you to a particular form of poetry and help you to find out how it works.

To show you a way of writing which strips words down to the bare minimum – and makes every word count.

To show you a way of suggesting rather than stating things.

To read 'between the lines' – thinking about the ways words and ideas connect with each other.

How? **With a partner**

Here is an example of a Haiku:

Not going in
but asking the price,
sheltering from the rain.

It has only three lines. Strictly speaking, there should be:

- five syllables in line one

- seven syllables in line two

- and five syllables in line three.

It is enough to get close to that and to think of syllables as sounds. If you break it up into sound units you get:

Not go-ing in   (4 sounds)
but ask-ing the price,   (5 sounds)
shel-t'ring from the rain. (5 sounds)

14 sounds, 11 words, 3 lines. And they tell a story to the reader who is prepared to do a little guessing.

This poem tells us that it is raining, that the person asks the price and the he/she does not go in. What sense can you make of that?

Work out answers to the following questions, then try to give the poem a short title – like a newspaper headline – which sums up what you think it is about:

- Why ask the price and not go in?

- Did the person ever mean to go in?

- What can you guess about this person's life?

Here is another example:

> Leaning upon staves
> and white haired – a whole family
> visiting the graves.

Work out an explanation for what is going on in the poem by answering the following questions, then give the poem a title which sums it up.

- What does the first line and a half tell you about these people?

- What does that word 'whole' in the second line tell you?

- What about where they are going? What does this tell you?

- Whose 'graves' might they be?

- What picture does the whole poem give you, and how do you feel about it?

Now read this Haiku, answer the questions and give it a title.

> Rain on a spring day:
> to the grove is blown a letter
> someone threw away.

- When you see the words 'spring day', what do you think of or expect it to be like?

- What does the idea of rain bring into that?

- Why might someone throw away a letter?

- What kind of letter might this one be?

- How could the four ideas:
     rain
     spring
     a letter
     thrown away
  all fit together to be parts of one idea?

- What sort of atmosphere does the whole thing have?

Now work out an explanation for each of the following three poems without any questions to help you. Then make up a two- or three-word title for each poem.

Making her doll
play younger sister –
the only child.

Glaring glumly at the sky
pecking at their packed lunch
at home.

Townsfolk, it is plain –
carrying red maple leaves
in the homebound train.

In a group

When you have finished, join another pair and talk together about the explanations that each of you has come up with and the titles you have invented for the poems.

124

Writing Haiku

What you do Experiment with writing Haiku of your own in three different ways.

Why? To use words clearly and economically to suggest more than they say.

   To try different approaches to find which one suits you best.

How? **(1) On your own**

Quickly write down what each of these suggests to you:

- a dripping tap
- a shadow on a wall
- a car's brakes screeching
- waves crashing on an empty beach
- breaking glass
- a door slamming.

Then shape the ideas you like best into Haiku, following the form as closely as you can.

125

(2) On your own

Jot down ideas for a story – just enough to get the idea clear in your mind. Then try to tell it in the form of a Haiku.

In a group

Read what you have written to the rest of your group. Listen while they tell you the story they think you were trying to tell. Then tell them your original idea.

Think about what they took from your poem and what you meant. Were there any differences?

Can you explain why any differences were there?

What changes can you make to your poem so that it does what you meant it to do?

(3) On your own

Write rough versions of three or four Haiku.

With a partner

Read each other's rough versions and then talk about them. Work the rough ideas into their final forms by:

- getting rid of unnecessary words or phrases
- making sure the words are clear and not vague.

Relations and relationships

The way we see it

What you do Write a group poem about a mother, father, sister or brother, and how they behave.

Why? To experiment with ways of describing people briefly.
To work on ways of linking ideas into groups, and linking groups into a complete piece of writing.

How? **In a group**

Read through this group poem to get an idea of what you need to do.

A YOUNGER BROTHER IS . . .

A brother is a robot
Acting like a toy
An interfering little pain
Destined to annoy.

A brother thinks he rules the world
And everything he owns
He seems to think he's superman
Yet wonders why Mum moans.

A brother says 'She hit me first'
'You're always blaming me'
A brother picks up words from dad
Like 'Where's my BLUDDY tea?'

A brother wants every toy
And every thing in sight
He's got his new red boxing gloves
But it's me who has to fight.

When he's asleep he's cute and sweet
With a smile upon his face
So let's forget his bad points
He's certainly no disgrace.

Nic, Nic and Melanie

A phrase introduces each group of lines:

A brother is/thinks/says/wants

and the group who wrote this poem chose to put in a set of balancing lines at the end.

As a group you need to decide whether you are going to write about a mother, a father, a sister or a brother. (A word of warning: if you decide to write about a brother or sister, agree beforehand whether you are writing about an older or younger one!)

Take the four introductory phrases and add any others you want to (A .... likes/hates, for instance) and, on your own, jot down whatever ideas you have for each one.

Discuss these together. Choose the ones you like best, put them into what seems a good order and find some ways of linking them together.

ACTIVITY 2

The family rules

What you do Put the set of 'Rules for Parents' printed opposite into what you think is their order of importance. Then work out your own 'Rules for Children'.

Why? To think about the rights and responsibilities of both children and adults.

To put forward and defend your point of view while listening to the views of others.

To explain, first in talk and then in writing, the reasons for some of your views.

How? **On your own**

Decide which of the 'Rules for Parents' you think are most likely to help parents and children to get on with each other. Do this by giving each rule a mark out of 5:

5 means very important, 4 means quite important, 3 means in between – you are not concerned one way or the other, 2 means not very important, 1 means not important at all.

With a partner

Compare the conclusions you have reached and discuss your reasons for them. Now work out ten or so 'Rules for Children'.

In a group

Get into groups of four. Discuss the rules you have made for children.

On your own

Choose three rules for children and three for parents which you think are especially important. Write a few sentences for each rule that you have chosen, explaining why you think it is important.

Parents should:

1   Help children with their homework if they get into difficulties.

2   Make decisions for their children about what friends they should have.

3   Make boys as well as girls do their share of the housework.

4   Allow children to have their own room and let the children keep it as they want to.

5   Allow children to watch whatever television programmes they like.

6   Make children earn their pocket money by doing agreed jobs.

7   Tell children the 'facts of life' and be frank with them.

8   Be on their children's side if anyone complains about them.

9   Listen to their children's points of view.

10   Insist that children are in bed by a certain time on weekdays.

11   Set rules for where their children can and cannot go.

12   Treat their children fairly (when there is more than one child in the family).

This page may be photocopied.

131

Relative horrors

What you do Discuss the pictures of the two aunts in the poems on pages 133–135 and the way that they have been created.

Why? To read the poems carefully and see what lies behind the words – what they *suggest* rather than what they say.

　　　　To put into your own words the picture that is presented to you in each poem.

　　　　To try to do in your own writing some of the things that the two poets do.

How?　　　**On your own**

As you read these poems, think about the character and nature of the aunt in each of them. Try to build up an idea of her:

● What does she look like?

● Is she big or small?

● Is she fat or thin?

● What does she wear?

● How does she talk?

Get as clear an idea as you can.

In a group

Share your ideas. Have you all got the same impression or different ones?

　　Where do your impressions come from? Find the lines, phrases or words in the poem that have made a particular suggestion to you.

　　Do your own experiences lead you to see the characters in a particular way?

On your own

Write a short pen-portrait based on one of your relatives. Do what the two poets have done here – exaggerate to produce an amusing picture.

132

BIG AUNT FLO

Every Sunday afternoon
She visits us for tea
And weighs-in somewhere between
A rhino and a flea.
   (But closer to the rhino!)

Aunt Flo tucks into doughnuts,
Eats fruit cake by the tin.
Her stomach makes strange noises
Just like my rude friend, Flynn.
   (Sounds more like a goat, really!)

Then after tea she heads for
The best chair in the room
And crashes on the cushions
With one resounding boom.
   (You'd think a door had slammed!)

Flo sits on knitting needles
And snaps them with a crack.
She squashes dolls and jigsaws
Behind her massive back.
   (And she doesn't feel a thing!)

But Aunt Flo learned a lesson,
There's no doubt about that,
Last Sunday when she grabbed the chair
And sat down on our cat.
   (Big Tom, a cat with a temper!)

The beast let out a wild yell
And dug his claws in . . . deep.
Poor Flo clutched her huge behind
And gave a mighty leap.
   (She almost reached the ceiling!)

So now at Sunday teatime
Jam doughnuts going spare.
Dad winks, and asks where Flo is.
While Tom sleeps on *that* chair.
   (And he's purring, the devil!)

Wes Magee

HUGGER MUGGER

I'd sooner be
Jumped and thumped and dumped,

I'd sooner be
Slugged and mugged . . . than *hugged* . . .

And clobbered with a slobbering
Kiss by my Auntie Jean:

You know what I mean:

Whenever she comes to stay,
You know you're bound

To get one.
A quick
   short
   peck
   would
   be
   OK.
But this is a
Whacking great
Smacking great
Wet one!

All whoosh and spit
And crunch and squeeze
And '*Dear* little boy!'
And 'Auntie's missed you!'
And 'Come to Auntie, she
Hasn't *kissed* you!'
Please don't do it, Auntie,
PLEASE!

Or if you've absolutely
Got to,

And nothing on *earth* can persuade you
Not to,

The trick
Is to make it
Quick,

You know what I mean?

For as things are,
I really would far,

Far sooner be
Jumped and thumped and dumped,

I'd sooner be
Slugged and mugged . . . than *hugged* . . .

And clobbered with a slobbering
Kiss by my Auntie

Jean!

Kit Wright

135

A family fight

What you do   Read the extract from 'Terry on the Fence' and then discuss the characters in it and their relationships. Retell the story in the passage from the point of view of one of the characters.

Why?   To look closely at how the writer has presented the characters.

To talk about different ways of seeing the same incident.

To consider your own and other people's opinions.

How?   **On your own**

Read the following passage from the opening of 'Terry on the Fence'. As you do so, pay particular attention to the three characters involved – Terry, his sister and their mother – and to their relationships: that is, the children with each other and each of them with their mother.

Decide what you think of the characters and how they behave towards each other.

In a group

Talk about your opinions of the characters and their behaviour. Keep looking back to the story to check that there is evidence to support your opinions.

Make a note of those conclusions you can agree about as well as any points about which there are differences of opinion, so that you can report back to the rest of the class.

On your own

Finally, retell the story from the point of view of:

- Terry
- *or* Tracey
- *or* Mrs Harmer.

In your writing you might imagine that whichever character you have chosen is telling a friend about what happened.

TERRY ON THE FENCE

As he got to the foot of the stairs his own full-length reflection in the hall mirror suddenly caught his approving eye. Oh yes! It really was a great shirt: he looked quite old in it, someone to be looked at twice. He stopped there, and putting his head slightly to one side, winked slowly at himself, the performer and the audience in one.

'Can I just keep it on till tea-time, Mum? My shirt?'

Mrs Harmer was pouring milk into another saucepan and trying to kick the fridge door shut at the same time.

'Yes,' she called back, long suffering. 'If you like . . .'

Terry puckered his lips at himself in the mirror, his head thrown back and his arms held wide for mass appreciation. The new discovery. Chart-buster. 'The Boy in the Black Shirt.' Frenzied applause and female screams of ecstasy filled his ears, and he waved to the cameras.

'You selfish little pig!'

Tracey had appeared at her bedroom door, her face twisted with disgust over the landing rail.

'Selfish little swank, you think you can get away with everything,' she spat at him. 'Mum, don't let him. Make him take it off.'

'Shut your mouth!' But Terry had learned long ago that you didn't shut Tracey up by standing and shouting at her. You took more direct action. He charged up the stairs with his head down, his feet drumming an angry tattoo on the tolerant treads. 'You shut up, Tracey! Keep your long nose out of it!' The swank bit had angered him, but her catching him posturing in front of the mirror had been worse; that was one of the biggest embarrassments of all.

Tracey stayed where she was long enough to see the strength of his reaction before diving for the shelter of her room. She knew that with her weight to the back of the door she could still withstand Terry's attacks, big as he was. But she just had time to yell, 'Mum! Mum! Tell Terry!'

Terry wasted no more words. He lunged for the top of the stairs and swung himself round the banister post on to the small landing in a practised movement which he'd perfected some years before in the long series of battles with Tracey. But she was no novice in that same theatre of war and her actions bore the hallmark of split-second timing. The door had slammed and Tracey had thrown herself against it before he made his furious assault.

'Chicken! Open the door! Let me in!'

'Mum!' came the muffled and breathless reply. 'Can you hear him?'

Mrs Harmer, who had certainly heard the thumping, the slamming and the shouts, was already on her way. In three or four angry strides she was at the foot of the stairs adding her own loud and unhappy comments to the commotion.

'You rotten kids!' she exploded. 'Can't you see I'm worn out enough as it is? All I ask is peace and quiet and a bit of doing what you're told. And all I get is this. Quarrel, quarrel, quarrel. Terry, come away from that door!'

She was half-way up the stairs, her head on a level with Terry's plimsolls through the banisters. It was just impossible to grab his ankles through the railings: she knew, she had tried often enough before. He stood there, his back to the door, his face red and angry, his eyes filling with tears of frustration.

'Rotten Tracey!' he said. 'It's her fault. She won't bloomin' leave me alone . . .'

Mrs Harmer reached the landing and knocked authoritatively on Tracey's door, while Terry, taking no chances, ducked his head in case the flailing hand was coming at him.

'Tracey, open this door. Come out here. I want a word with you.'

Mrs Harmer wiped the door with her sleeve where she had smeared it with the raspberry powder from an Instant Whip. 'Come on, hurry up.'

The door opened a cautious crack to reveal Tracey's pale but righteous face.

'Tell him, Mum . . .'

'Come out here.'

'He's nothing but a rotten selfish pig. He thinks he can get away with anything, just because he's a boy. You used to be much more strict with me . . .'

Tracey stood back in her room, holding the door open, in a compromise position of safety both from Terry's foot and her mother's hand.

'Tracey, how many times have I told you not to cause trouble? We'd live a nice peaceful life if you'd just keep your remarks to yourself. Leave him

138

alone. You're not his mother, I am. I'll deal with him if I have to. It's none of your business.'

'That's right,' said Terry, pleased to see his sister getting ticked-off.

'And you!' Mrs Harmer suddenly turned and shouted at him, her patience completely exhausted. Her face showed all the strain of late nights, of trying to run a home and of doing a full-time job, as she returned to a familiar theme. 'All I ever ask of you children is that you behave yourselves and mind your own business, and that's all you can ever not do . . .' She was too tired and fed up with them to put it any better. 'If you can't get on with one another, keep out of each other's way for God's sake! I've got enough on my plate without stupid quarrelling kids! And the sooner you two realize it the better.'

There was a moment's pause while Mrs Harmer's shouted remarks rang round the small landing, sinking in, before she shifted her weight ready to return to the milk downstairs. She sighed. Another crisis over.

But Tracey was unable to resist the temptation to have the last word. 'He gets away with murder,' she said in a low sulky voice as she began to shut her door.

'I do not!' Terry lunged at her but he was a slam too late and the hardboard panelling took the force of his battering hands.

'Stop it!' shrieked Mrs Harmer. She was really angry with them now, and frustrated at the situation suddenly getting out of control with so much to do and so little time before Jack came in.

'Spoilt little baby!'

'I'm not!' Terry deeply resented Tracey calling him a baby. She had always held her two year's seniority over him like some sort of debt he owed her.

'Yes you are, Mamma's little baby!'

'I'm not!'

'Where's 'our dummy, 'ickle baby?'

'Shut up!'

'Change 'is nappy, then?'

'You're asking for it!'

Mrs Harmer's shrieking voice reached a new high. '"Stop it!" I said.'

'That's what you are! A little baby!'

'No I'm bloody not!'

That was the limit for Mrs Harmer. She whacked at Terry's head and caught him a stinging slap on the left ear. She was already furious and shaking as a result of the total disregard from the pair of them, and now she was both shocked and ashamed at hearing one of her own thoughtless swear-words coming back from the boy. Somehow she always imagined that he didn't hear what he wasn't supposed to. Perhaps it was because he had never copied them in her hearing before.

'How dare you? I'm not having that, Terry Harmer, not from a little boy like you.'

Tracey opened her door again, disappointed at having missed the climax. But the sight of Terry in tears and holding the side of his head told her all she wanted to know. A faint smile and a knowing look crept onto her face, an expression on tiptoe ready to vanish the moment her mother looked round at her.

'You've gone too far. I know I'll never go to heaven for what I sometimes say, but that's no reason for you to start using bad language. Tracey's right, I give you too much of your own way. You wore that shirt when I definitely told you not to, and now you start coming the old soldier up here . . .'

Tracey's smile broadened and settled complacently on her face as she turned back into her room, her task of bringing Terry to book seemingly completed. She left the door wide open so that Terry would know that she was hearing it all while she brushed her hair at the dressing-table and hummed softly to herself.

Mrs Harmer went on, a bit more like a mother now instead of an angry woman. She was quickly calming down now that Terry had put her in control of the situation once more: and there was also the undoubted satisfaction of having clouted someone for the frustrations of the past five minutes.

'You're still my little boy, Terry Harmer, and while you're in my house you'll do as I say and you'll act decent. Now is that clear? Is it?'

She stood with her hands on her hips, leaning forward, her eyes boring into him. Terry, his head still ringing with the unlucky blow, and his eyes full with both the pain and the hurt of the injustice, felt his stomach suddenly leap over in angry rebellion. That's it! He pushed past his mother. He had had enough. To hell with the consequences. He didn't care any more. It was the sort of extreme mood he's seen kids in at school when they'd shouted at a teacher. He thumped loudly down the stairs and snatched up his duffel bag from the bottom banister post.

'Terry!'

'I'm clearing off! No one wants me in this house. All you do is just shout at me and treat me like a baby . . .' He got to the front door, almost too choked to shout the words out. 'So I'm leaving. For good!' He threw the door shut behind him with all the force he could muster, clattering the letterbox and starting the wind-up bell ringing.

The slam shook through the house as slams always did, but tonight, being tonight, it carried through to the kitchen in just sufficient strength to stir the crockery in the sink. With a shifting, settling clatter the china pyramid collapsed, sending the milky saucepan bouncing off the rim of the sink to clang loudly across the kitchen floor, spreading a pool of dirty white water with it. For Gladys Harmer it almost drowned Terry's parting shot. But not quite. Anger and frustration had lent power to his vocal chords. He pushed open the letter-box flap and yelled at them both at the top of his voice.

'Bloody good-bye!'

Bernard Ashley

Your own writing

What you do Write about relatives and relationships in any form you choose.

Why? To capture a particular person or relationship in words.
  To practise the writing skills you have been developing throughout this book.

How? **On your own**

Choose one of these topics:

1 Describe any one of your relatives in the setting which seems most suitable for him/her.

2 Describe an argument between a sister and brother or between a child and one of his/her parents.

3 Suppose:
  ● a girl or boy has come in much later than she/he promised
  ● *or* has failed to tidy her/his room despite promising to do so
  ● *or* has to explain that she/he has got into trouble at school.

  Write – as a play-script, if you choose – the conversation with her/his mother or father.

4 You will have seen advertisements for all sorts of things on television, in newspapers and in magazines. Using whatever ideas you can from these, write an advertisement of your own, headed 'Relative for sale'. Choose one of your relatives, or make one up. Try to produce something really funny.

Answers

Unit 4, Activity 4 (pages 51, 52 and 54)

The middle three verses of 'Queen Nefertiti' are:

Over the pavement
Her feet go clack;
Her legs are as tall
As a chimney stack;

Her fingers flicker
Like snakes in the air;
The walls split open
At her green-eyed stare;

Her voice is as thin
As the ghosts of bees;
She will crumble your bones,
She will make your blood freeze.

The remaining verses of 'Mixed Brews' are:

She practised her charms
By waving her arms
And muttering words and curses;
And every spell
Would have worked out well
If she hadn't mixed the verses.

Not long since,
When she wanted a prince
To wake the sleeping beauty
A man appeared
With a long grey beard,
Too old to report for duty!

When she hoped to save
Aladdin's Cave
From his uncle cruel and cranky,
She concocted a spell
That somehow fell
Not on him but on Widow Twanky.

With a magic bean
She called for a Queen
Who was locked in the wizard's castle.
There came an old hag
With a postman's bag
And threepence to pay on the parcel.

What comes of a witch
Who has hitch after hitch?
I'm afraid that there's no telling:
But I think as a rule
She returns to school
And tries to improve her spelling.

In order, the missing verbs in 'The Witch's Cat' are:

wrote   Going   was   weren't   trickled   stamped   broke   leaving   has

Unit 6, Activity 2 (page 79)
Set out in its original form, the poem 'The Snow' reads:

In no way that I chose to go
Could I escape the falling snow.
I shut my eyes, wet with my fears:
The snow still whispered at my ears.
I stopped my ears in deaf disguise:
The snow still fell before my eyes.
Snow was my comrade, snow my fate,
In a country huge and desolate.
My footsteps made a shallow space,
And then the snow filled up the place,
And all the walking I had done
Was on a journey not begun.

Unit 8, Activity 2 (page 101)
Michael Rosen set out Sections 9 to 12 of 'Nightmare' like this:

Can't someone give me a hand up?
Can't you see?
I'm between the lines
and the train's coming
give me a hand someone
give me a hand
the train's coming
give me a hand
I can't climb up
the train's coming

and the platform's sliding in towards me too
with the train still coming
coming down the tunnel
the platform's sliding
sliding in towards me too.

I'm still down
Can't anyone see me
down between the lines?

Look
see
me
the train
the platform
me
the train
near now
nearer now
nearer and nearer now
NOW

That's all.

Unit 10, Activity 1 (pages 113 to 115)

A = 3, B = 7, C = 1, D = 8, E = 6, F = 5, G = 4, H = 2